Writers of the Loam

A Writers' Rooms Community Anthology

Jill Cronbaugh, Nicholas Lee, & Rachel J. Sharkey, eds.

First edition, 2023.
The Writers' Rooms
Iowa City, IA
welcome@thewritersrooms.org

Cover design is by: Jill Cronbaugh

Cover art: *Alice* by Jordan Cronbaugh

ISBN: 978-0-578-59474-3

To the writers of the community who make The Writers' Rooms
possible…thank you.

Table of Contents

Cover: *Alice* by Jordan Cronbaugh

Introduction by Erin Casey

About The Writers' Rooms
Donations

Introduction

Dear Reader, thank you for your support of The Writers' Rooms (TWR)! By picking up this book, you have joined our creative community. This book is our way to celebrate you and to thank everyone for helping our dream of the Rooms come to life.

TWR is an organization which endeavors to create a safe, inclusive community for all writers. We believe that everyone has a wealth of knowledge and a story to share. In our Rooms we bring both to the table. These community-led meetings include a myriad of craft discussions, prompts, lessons, and time to socialize and write. Our events, which are usually held in conjunction with local businesses and libraries, offer a safe space in which to meet other members of your local writing community.

Our Rooms would not exist were it not for the incredible writers throughout the creative corridor, as well as our dedicated and brilliant Concierges, the leaders of our Rooms. We've watched new writers learn from seasoned minds. Authors with writer's block have found a way to flourish and venture into their literary world once again. Most importantly, people have found a Room to call home, a place where they feel safe to share their voice and find help when they struggle.

The stories, poetry, and art you're about to experience are from our community. We are writers helping writers who endeavor to share each others' voices. We chose the theme of earth for this anthology to complete our elemental journey.

Just remember, no matter where you are in your writing journey, you are never alone. You have a community waiting for you.

Best,
Erin Casey

The Night Gardener

Madeleine Kleppinger

"Are you getting a puppy?" Cathy pointed her saggy, pale fingers at the new fence surrounding her neighbor's yard.

Nora took her time stretching out her back and tightening her cinnamon-colored ponytail. She'd been hunched over the peonies for the past twenty-five minutes dusting every leaf with antifungal powder. The blooms were magnificent this year and she planned to ensure the same next season.

"You've been working in your yard a lot lately. And getting that fence installed, sure was a lot of mess—"

Cathy thought everything was a mess. The leaves, rainstorms, grass clippings, neighbors who had parties on Saturday evenings.

"No puppy, Cathy," Nora cut her off. She checked her phone hoping Cathy would get the message to go away.

"Well, if you had wanted one, Don would have gotten used to the barking. He'd just have been cranky about it."

"You won't have to worry about barking or puppy poop or anything," Nora's smile was so tight it pulled at the stitches along her temple that she kept turned away from prying eyes. "I just wanted some privacy."

She tossed her gardening tools into the work bucket at her left and retreated through the gate behind her new privacy fence. Even at nine thirty-eight at night, Cathy still had a comment. Trying to avoid her neighbors' opinions, Nora had convinced herself that gardening at night in a place like Tennessee was just practical. The heat and humidity could knock a person flat. And it was a good way to wind down after a long day at the office.

Night gardening had also become Nora's only option after a suspicious mole on her cheek had sent her to the dermatologist a week ago.

"We better biopsy that," the doctor had said. "Someone your age shouldn't have face lumps like those."

The doctor looked through images sent back from the lab during her follow up appointment. "These cells are definitely malignant." Nora couldn't tell what was cancer and what wasn't.

"Are you enjoying your new facelift? One of the perks, I'm told.

I did have to cut some pretty wide margins," Dr. Pietras said.

Nora's eyes were fixed on the top right corner or the lab images, "female/Caucasian/33 yrs."

Cancer before fifty. Cancer before marriage. Cancer before children. Cancer before her mortgage was paid off. Cancer before she'd even ever had a fender bender in rush hour traffic. She and her best friend had just been complaining about adulting last week. How was this happening?

The pamphlet in her post-op care bag said, "NO SUN EXPOSURE – 3 WEEKS"

Three weeks would be hard for someone who went walking during every lunch break and practically raced home to work in their garden. Hard, but not impossible. And staying locked away inside would prevent anybody from asking about the massive bandage on her face. She coordinated her work meetings around the biopsy date and set her email signature status to "Working from Home." No one had to know.

By day four post operation, Nora was feeling practically batty waiting around for the wound to close. She lifted sloppy spoonfuls of oatmeal and berries fantasizing about the rich loam around the roots of her mulberry bushes. She was desperate to pinch every wilted petunia and marigold and begonia bloom. Her ears craved the song of the cicada choir perched outside high up in her ash trees. If only she could, she would raise a hallelujah with them. Or at least stop the pleading cries of the spent vinca blooms beyond her office window. What could fifteen minutes spent deadheading really do?

Dr. Pietras' nasally reminder as he patted her cheek, "These steroids I am putting you on make you prone to sunburn, and that's not what our skin needs right now."

On the fifth night, Nora stood in her foyer armed with her trusted flathead screwdriver and a sprung-open set of garden shears as the sun slid below the tree line. Eight thirty-nine, sundown. The enemy was a headlight yellow dandelion thriving in the dead center of Nora's shaggy lawn. The yolk-colored devil had mocked her since midmorning when she spotted it on the way to the kitchen for a coffee refill. It had been impossible to focus on anything else all afternoon.

Under protection of night, Nora plunged the screwdriver deep into the rich soil of her tended lawn. Metal bit into the dandelion root. Nora had been overeager and now she wouldn't be able to get the whole thing out. The broken root extracted from the earth pronounced it would be back.

But so would Nora. As the sunless evening air kissed her paling skin, the darkness set her free.

It was the overhead garage lights that alerted Cathy to Nora's new nocturnal patterns. As the unappointed neighborhood patrol, Cathy couldn't rest without some sort of explanation for this change. What had started out as simple questioning that Nora expertly deflected turned into Cathy lingering. First it was milling about outside in the late afternoon heat around the time the mail courier made his rounds. But Nora was a millennial, she didn't check the mail on time.

Then Nora had seen Cathy sneak over to her front porch after a package was delivered, pretending to pick it up and walk it back to Nora's house like it was delivered to the wrong address. Nora ignored the knocking and Cathy eventually left the package on the stoop.

A confrontation was unavoidable by day eight. It was cruel to avoid the woman when Cathy had something so obviously on her mind. Nora didn't want her stitches to be noticed, lest everyone in the whole community would be stopping by to see their poor little neighbor. She peeled off the bandage and let down her hair. Even though the waves were kinked from the elastic, Nora let her hair fall forward to cover the stitches in her almond hued skin. Breath in, and out.

Cathy swung wide her screen door four point three seconds later and dashed toward Nora holding limp roses cut days before. "Nora, I cut you some roses. I know you didn't get your bushes winterized properly before the freeze last year."

"Thanks, Cathy," Nora ignored the flowers extended toward her. She would afford Cathy exactly the amount of time it would take Nora to look at each piece of mail that she was picking out one letter at a time.

"You've been up so late recently," Cathy's voice edged with—

What was that? Nora wondered. Annoyance? Fake concern?

"Don told me to offer if you need help with anything."

"No need." Nora kept her head bowed reading a TruGreen® ad in the stack of mail. The smiling, mowing man felt like a taunt. Why would she need an advertisement for lawn service? Her grass was perfect. They should have seen that for themselves.

Cathy edged closer. "Don offered to fix a few things while you are at work. Then we can all have some peace and quiet."

"You shop at Aldi's?" Nora waved a coupon flyer from the grocery store, "great ads this week."

Cathy's gaudy pink toes grazed Nora's pristine perfect edging.

"Of course, I don't shop at Aldi's. The better grocery is Kroger."

Nora flicked the postcard into the waste bin that she poised at the ready on the curb. All junk mail, but Cathy needed a stronger message. Nora refused to make eye contact with the woman.

"It's just that our bedroom window faces this side of your garage—"

Nora felt a cool wetness on her cheek. She resisted the urge to touch the wound with Cathy standing there yammering on. The stitches must have pulled. Nora handed over the TruGreen® flyer to Cathy without a word. Truth be told, Don was falling behind on his lawn care.

The rose-colored hue of her cheeks was a mix between the weeping sutures and the heat of embarrassment. Nora hadn't said much of anything in the week following the surgery. There was no need. She slipped into a silent existence with ease. Everyone at work seemed quite alright to communicate over email. Even her mom had been satisfied with the ambiguous and cheerful texts that Nora had sent. It wasn't that she didn't like people. Her skin crawled when people's eyes fixed on her. Sometimes it felt like everyone needed something from Nora, and she didn't have it. Whatever it even was. She was still figuring that out for herself.

"Cathy, I've got a work call I have to get on."

Night after night, Nora followed the moonlight going from one side of the yard to the other. Just like one might follow shade to stay cool during the day. She found she could work with the lights off, her hands and eyes becoming more adept to working in the dark, and that kept Cathy from raising any more complaints.

The dermatologist examined the pink, puckered skin on Nora's cheekbone and jawline at the three-week appointment.

"Healing, yes, but we best keep an eye on it." His feather-soft touch tilted Nora's chin, so he might analyze the new skin in the light. "Come see me in six weeks. Unless something changes. Stay out of the sun."

Stay out of the sun. No problem, doc.

Nora was starting to enjoy the time alone. Deadheading and uprooting dandelions turned into pruning and shaping shrubs over the weeks. The time passing by unnoticed. Nora had become so familiar with her lawn; it was arguable that she spent more time outside than in. And it was in those long midnight hours that a vision in the mist condensing over the grass came into her mind. The moonlight fractured in the dew drops, twinkling like a million bright stars. Nora reflected on creating a reflection pond, dead center of her lawn. If she planned it right, it would cast a perfect picture of the Milky Way.

A need so great bloomed inside her gut. To bring the moon down to earth was an enormous task. Right now, she needed to believe that she could accomplish big things. She paced out a ten-foot diameter. The moon's reflection was bigger. She extended the edge to fifteen feet. The moon's shadow was contained, edge to edge. Only seven hundred six-and five tenths square feet. She imagined the number in her mind. Dr. Pietras said a patient only had to go two years of clear checkups before they were fully in remission. Seven hundred thirty days. Healing had a perimeter. Just like her mole had been cut out with clean margins.

Nora scurried to the garage for a shovel. It was only twelve thirty-seven. She could at least dig the hole tonight and fill it tomorrow before the full moon was gone.

Shink!

Spade to soil. Each thud of earth landing in the wheelbarrow sent a shiver through her body. This pond would be magnificent. It would be breathtaking. She could just see black velvet koi swimming in the shallows creating graceful ripples of moonlight. White lily pads would look like the Northern Star and all her constellations. And the jeweled armor of bright goldfish would glint majestically as a natural treasure trove.

Beads of sweat pearled at Nora's brow and atop the curve of her upper lip. A tinge of chemical burn tightened the skin of her temple. The muscles of her arms sagged. How could the wheelbarrow be full again? She couldn't fathom lifting it to dump it into the compost pile out back.

Nora felt a heavy wetness along her chin. The back of her hand came away rust red. Soil and sweat and blood. The delicate new skin had popped open. The instant reaction of nausea from an empty stomach told Nora that she had overworked herself. An electronic beep from her watch chimed for morning. Just beyond the end of the lane, a canary yellow orb split the sky. Instant warmth grazed Nora's cheek. For a moment she leaned into it.

"Stay out of the sun."

Her heart squeezed. She couldn't leave her yard in this state. There was dirt mound from when she had stopped bothering to take the wheelbarrow loads to the compost hours ago. Shovels and picks laid about. Her boots were caked in mud. Surely the neighbors would think she had gone mad now. Nora made a mad dash into the house for a hat and sun shirt.

In the shadows of the house, she could barely make out her features in the hallway mirror. But she put together with the slight bit of sunlight that she was an absolute disaster. Rubbing away grime from her cheeks made things worse. She settled with pulling her wild hair into a ponytail and strapping her hat low on her brow. Nora dashed back to clean up the evidence.

Five neighbors stood on the sidewalk. No one moved.

Don, Cathy, the two daybreak walkers who pumped their arms in rhythm every morning, and Robert. They had seen her emerge from her front door before she had seen them. Even if she melted into a puddle on the front stoop, she imagined they would still be determined to ask her what in the world she was doing.

Robert, the single man from three doors down who refused to run with a shirt on, looked caught in the headlights. Like maybe he hadn't planned to be standing outside of her house this morning. Or maybe he had finally paused long enough to wonder where his shirt was. But now that he was here, he was one of them.

His bare chest steamed. And so did his espresso colored hair. It gave off the impression that he was fresh baked, and Nora wondered if he might also taste like gingerbread.

"Nora, we heard you working last night," Cathy approached like she might a dog whose ears were laid back. Unaccompanied, she halted and shot a glaring look at her husband.

"Cathy thought you were out burying somebody," Don said. Cathy rolled her eyes, thin lips pinched.

Everyone was staring at the sinkhole in Nora's front lawn.

"I'm installing a pond," Nora offered, despite it being none of their business. "Really a pet project. Like owning a betta fish in a bowl."

"Honey, this looks more like you are planning a swimming hole," one of the walkers moved in sizing up the development while adjusting the Velcro® of her visor.

Nora's throat was gathering a film of mucus. She attempted to clear her throat, but the sound came out like a growl and Cathy jumped. Nora was too tired to care. Her yard was a disaster, and she was supposed to be punching in for work in two hours. She squared her petite shoulders to lift the full wheelbarrow.

"Whatever you are working on," Robert said, one earbud poised to be returned to his head, "it's going to look great."

Nora shrugged her shoulders to adjust the weight of the

compost she was lifting. As Robert jogged off, she stole one more look at the muscles in his back. How did someone even get those?

The rest of the week, every evening when Nora made her way outside, Don was milling about on his driveway swatting at fireflies that got too close. Even if she sent him away, Cathy would send him right back outside. Nora was going to have to wait them out.

It became a little routine, Don trying to find things to do to look busy. Nora turning on the evening news hoping the light would convince them both that she would be staying inside. A few times she waited so long only to fall asleep in her armchair, scrambling awake the following morning to the ring of multiple alarms.

Each morning that Nora failed to get back out to her front yard, the unfinished hole mocked her from the view of her office desk. If only Don had a spine. They all knew he didn't want to be out there, but Cathy had put her husband up to the task of meddling. The older couple would have to give up eventually.

Dandelions sprouted up in the Kentucky Blue grass like itched chicken pox. Ivy crowded the base of Nora's ornamental Japanese Maple. And the mud that washed out of the basin she had created was weighing down the petunia petals causing them to wilt and die.

It took nine days before Don did not appear outside after dinner.

Nora donned a black tracksuit that night and tucked her hair into the collar at the nape of the neck. The supplies for the pond, packed with discretion, had been delivered earlier in the week. While waiting for Don to give up, Nora had browsed countless tutorial videos on pond installation. She was ready.

Stepping into her overgrown garden was like greeting old friends. A little ditty hummed across Nora's lips. A full evening of unsolicited aloneness spanned before her. It had been a rough week and half cooped up inside.

Nora was still on sun restrictions and had spent her return week at the office deflecting the multitude of concerned onlookers. Her sarcastic humor did most of the heavy lifting, but she was weary from all of the questions. If only people could just mind their own business. She offered them the same courtesy every day. Nora brushed the tension and stress away with the soil on her hands. The pit was exactly the right shape. And deep enough for twenty koi.

Footsteps thudded on the pavement behind her, and she whipped around ready to face an attacker. Robert seized back, and his hands yanked the earbuds from his ears. Nora cowered into her hole hoping he hadn't caught sight of her.

"Wow! I did not see you there," he panted.

Nora had never seen a man's legs sweat before, but there were Robert's calves at her eye level. His lean muscles flexed in the moonlight.

His watch chirped while he messed with the buttons, she had cut his run time short. Nora hoped he would plug his earbuds back in and take up his pace. And his ankles tensed to do so, until he doubled over clamping large palms over his shins.

"Shit, splints!"

He toppled into the grass inches from Nora's nose and the hole. Robert rolled about in a strained happy baby pose. He howled.

"Uh, I don't know how to help you—"

"Ice, please, ice," he gasped and writhed.

She scrambled out of the pit, jolted into action by his pleading, and ran to the house. Inside she flung back cabinet doors and drawers searching for something to hold the entire contents of an ice tray. She spotted a crumpled t-shirt laying on her mudroom floor from Monday evening's yoga session.

"Gross," Nora held the limp fabric to her nose and resigned. "What the fuck."

She heard a mewling from outside her kitchen window that caused her to look and scatter fifty ice pellets across her kitchen island. She scrambled to gather most of them into a ball of her Classic Cruisers tee shirt. The situation was deteriorating the way the thin cotton from the father daughter-weekend seventeen years ago was.

Robert was still rocking himself on the front lawn when she made it outside. Tears rolled down his temples and for a moment Nora paused to wonder what it would be like to dab them up with a kitchen towel.

The front screen shut behind her with a metallic clang. Robert looked up and extended his hand, "Oh my gosh, you are a hero."

He crushed the makeshift ice pack to his shins, his eyes closed tight to the new sensation of freezing flesh. He was hot. Like a kind boss who gives his VIP parking spot to the pregnant woman at the office kind of hot. And for whatever reason, Nora cared so much about him being in pain.

"I've gotten these since I was a kid."

Nora had to shake herself from this ridiculous daydream. Her brain raced to say something normal.

"So, why keep punishing yourself?"

"I love being out here at twilight," A brilliant smile spread from ear to ear, eclipsing the pained expression on his forehead. Behind Robert's closed eyes, he was picturing a young man running through a field all alone.

"No one around to ask you questions or interrupt your thoughts," his green eyes peered through squinted eyelids, "usually no one to see you collapse in pain and bawl like a baby."

"I saw no such thing."

He fell back, arms long enough to hold the ice in place. Long enough to wrap her up.

"Sorry for gawking at your pet project the other day, but Cathy kept sending Don over to the house. The poor man just wants to watch a baseball game."

Nora chortled, "In peace."

They laughed for a moment, letting their breaths fall in the space between them.

"I feel like an asshole."

Nora studied his face. What was he about to say?

"You are too nice, Nora. I bet people are always taking advantage of that without even realizing it. Like me, of all the yards I could have collapsed in, I am in yours. I'm crawling around trying to see behind your privacy fence."

Nora perked up. She might be taking the hot card back.

"Metaphorically, but I am taking advantage of your kindness. You're one of those gals who just does nice things for people." He grimaced at the ache in his leg, "even when they are rolling about on your beautiful lawn whining."

"And pretending to know me, too," Nora said.

Robert smiled, and just as quickly she caught a tinge of concern in his eyes as he looked at her cheek. It was enough truth for her to realize, it wasn't just the doctors. Or her. To anyone with a sharp eye, her skin wasn't healing the way healthy skin should. She needed to face the truth.

So, she climbed out of the in-progress pond. And for whatever reason she decided to tell him.

"It's melanoma." She kept her fingers down at her side. The reflex was hard to fight, but she refused to let her hand rise to her face and graze the unhealing scar.

Robert lolled his head onto his propped-up fist. His eyes asked questions she had no answers for.

Why was he so okay with this awkward silence? And how had he been so quick to believe that she was nice to people? She had always thought of herself as standoffish. If only the pond were full, Nora would dive into it and be swallowed whole.

"Nora, you and I," he held a beat, "who else are we going to tell our stuff to?"

His eyes held miniature moons in them. Bright white crescents signaling the start of the new lunar cycle.

"It's not healing, either," she trialed.

A flicker of gold swam in his iris. And the little creases at the corners gathered wetness just before he blinked.

"Go ahead, Nora," he said, "we have time and I want to listen."

"There isn't a lot to say. I mostly hated being stuck inside waiting to heal," a finger tap to the wound, "or to get a fatal diagnosis."

Her cells were changing on the surface and within her veins and bones and lymph nodes. And what she wanted most was to leave behind good, healthy cells where her own had failed. It was the most important thing to Nora that the cancer cells that were dividing in her body would quickly be outnumbered by all the fern and mushroom and koi cells she was adding to her garden every night.

"I name stars," Robert started, "in the NASA registry. You can have stars discovered in the galaxy named for things, or people."

He relaxed into the grass, letting his leg rest on the ice pack.

"But I don't name the stars after myself. I use markers from major events in my life. Things no one else would know about because I experienced them alone. Those things that happened to me, they did matter, though. Energy and intention and thoughts. Even if it is just for me. When I look up at the stars, they tell a history that otherwise would have been lost by my solitude."

He was staking a claim on his singleness. Proof he was more than okay being alone. Nora felt solidarity fill her core. Tending her garden at night was her created history. Each plant marked a night of her solitude battling worries and concerns about her recent diagnosis. And also, the nights she had enjoyed by herself.

"Robert?"

"Mmmhmm?" his gaze remained fixed skyward.

"Can I know the name of a star?"

"August in McKinley."

His fingertips held his leg. Not the shin splints, but an old injury was flaring up and prodding his mind.

"I went there to let go. More than I should have."

The weight of his past pressed her down into the grass. Her eyes searched the indigo blue sky, the stars were starting to give way to daybreak. As she craned her neck searching for the only witnesses of Robert's darkest night, the crown of her head brushed his. He didn't move away.

"Point it out, I want to see it before the sun comes up."

Nora could feel him search the galaxy from her angle. Grass tickled the thin skin at her temple but it didn't hurt and so she didn't flinch. Sensation was a good thing. Sensation meant living cells dividing and growing and healing.

"In Denali, you see more stars than you can count. One night, they were so bright I couldn't fall asleep. I unzipped my tent's fly and found another reason to be bothered to live. The Milky Way, it was so beautiful. And then it became, what if I had that many reasons to live?"

"It got easier to think up reasons the longer I pushed myself." Robert guffed, "Which seems crazy. But once I got going, I couldn't stop. Nieces, favorite foods, countries to visit on my bucket list, marathon fees I'd already paid."

Nora laughed despite the gravity of the conversation, "You're living for bills?"

"I didn't think I'd have to explain my need for finishing projects to a woman who landscapes at midnight."

The tension broke, and the two erupted. Robert liked Nora's laugh, another reason.

"So, a pond?"

"To reflect your stars."

Robert rolled over, his face tilted unabashedly close to Nora's lips.

"The real reason."

It had been so long since she had been this close to another person. Breaking eye contact would mean a retreat to safety and even though her body ached for it a small pinprick of gold in Robert's eyes made her wait. She had never watched a sunrise in someone else's eyes before.

"Originally there wasn't a reason. One night the moon was so big and beautiful. And I was feeling selfish and wanted it for myself. Why shouldn't I get something nice for my garden during my last few days on earth?"

His smile deepened, "Shall I lasso you the moon, Mary?"

"Don't tease, George," Nora pulled back under the guise of the joke. She wasn't sure how to explain this great need to control her environment. Slow down time.

Robert sensed the retreat. He wasn't ready to give up this closeness. He needed to know why Nora believed she had been selfish. He'd been a fool to push into her vulnerable spaces so quickly. Good grief he was sprawled out on her lawn, icing his shins with a pack made by her t-shirt.

"Nora, can I come back tomorrow night and finish the pond with you?"

How could she say no? She was the nice girl after all.

The next day, Nora regretted every whim she ever had about Robert. Her stomach knotted and unknotted. She tore apart her closet looking for any un-shabby, hole-less work clothes that she might have. At ten, she braided her hair. At noon, she put it in a ponytail. At three, she tussled it during a virtual training until it was limp. At six forty-five, she floofed the knotted locks into a messy bun. Nothing felt right.

Around dusk, she couldn't stand waiting any longer. She slathered on sunscreen bemoaning the greasy look of her cheekbones in the hallway mirror. Her hands needed something to do, and this was her only ticket to the outside.

Within the hour, Nora's mind settled. Her thoughts creeping and anchoring in place, like ivy along a brick wall. The flowers unfurled in the cooling evening temperatures enveloping her in a beautiful perfume. Nora imagined her plants near the future pond basking in the humidity rising from the water's surface. And she had brought all of it together.

Robert was jogging down the block toward her front yard. He hadn't forgot, unfortunately. At least this time he came wearing a shirt. Nora scrambled to feign busyness. Maybe he'd get the hint and call it an early night.

"It smells incredible out here!" Robert said.

"Thanks. Hey, you know," Nora searched for an easy way to let him off the hook.

Robert was staring at her, eyes wide. "Nora, I am really glad to be here. I really enjoyed talking with you last night."

He couldn't mean that. And she wasn't sure she should have even told him all of those things. "Robert, I've learned to be really suspicious of these things."

"What do you mean?"

"These types of feelings," Nora sighed at the explanation of it all. "The falling hard and fast because things-look-so-bleak-kind-of-feelings."

"Good thing these aren't those kinds of feelings," he was actually relaxing. Like he knew Nora was going to say these exact words to him. "Have you ever thought about my running route?"

"Um, no, Mr. Vanity," Nora chopped at the edging line, "and also, how lonely do you think I am?"

If admitting she was dying wasn't a fall hard and fast kind of scenario, Nora didn't know what qualified—

"I ended up on your front lawn, wallowing around in self-pity disguised as shin-splints long before you told me your sob story about having cancer. I even offered to help dig your little burial plot here."

Nora took in the scene around them. They were standing at the edge of a six-foot-deep pit, near about the width of a grown person.

"This isn't a burial plot," Nora gushed, cheeks blooming cranberry red.

"No," Robert smirked, "just a reflection pond for reflecting on your untimely death."

She launched the shovel full of dirt at him not expecting the thwack of mud clod meeting his skull.

"Oh my gosh, I'm so sorry!"

"No you aren't and stop it. The smile was worth it."

Robert snagged a shovel leaning against a pile of soil, "Thanks for getting me a tool." He smirked and Nora learned that he loved being right.

"As I was saying, my house, and route, are that direction." He pointed the spade tip opposite of Nora's front door. "But I started running the extra zero point one mile because one spring morning I caught a whiff of lilacs that I couldn't help but follow right here. And low and behold, a Garden of Eden. And in a moment, it all made sense."

"Here lives a woman who needs a life," Nora quipped.

"Why all the neighbors talk about you."

And there it was again. A bloom on Nora's cheeks that surpassed the brilliant red geraniums in the window boxes. Her edger bit into the grass roots sending her stumbling forward.

Robert kept on, "They are jealous of the joy you create every day. I figured a woman who didn't even notice all the hubbub she was causing must have created a true sanctuary. Somewhere I wanted to spend the start of my every day. And then to my delight that woman, she is more stunning than her garden."

He slipped the last sentence in just at audible level, testing the delicate space between them.

Nora's lashes fluttered closed. It occurred to her that she was trying to make her world smaller so she could handle everything that felt too big. Her diagnosis. Her to do lists. These new feelings for Robert. Even the moon.

With everything small, then her fears could be small. She'd spent so much of her life being afraid and she was tired of it. No one had ever told her the fortress that eased her anxiety was also beautiful to them. The true mark of her good times and energy, they were beautiful and worthy.

"I once read that every flower is a love story," she started. To her right side she sensed Robert lean in on her shovel. "And what sounds better than living in a place surrounded by love stories?"

Her hands had stilled, and his body had stopped moving earth.

"The other night," Robert said, "I wondered why now? We've lived on this block together how many—"

She stopped him, "I might know this one."

And they kept digging until it was time to lay the rock and bedding. And they splashed one another with water while the pond filled. Taking every hour of the night back for themselves.

Because the reason didn't really matter. Now was when they wanted to be together.

It wasn't long before everyone in the neighborhood was talking about the out-of-towners who'd bought Robert's house for an absolute steal. What had he been thinking, giving up a property like that? But Nora and Robert wouldn't know that because they were busy feeding the koi and looking for the stars they had named on the registry. One for every moment they had chosen to share.

Resilience
Spike Dawkins

Getting to Know Worms
Diane DeBok

I was new to the practice of keeping a bin of composting redworms in my basement, so when I lifted the lid to check on them and found most of them crawling up the sides to escape, it was an oh shit moment. I clapped the lid back on and went to my computer for some fast research.

For the first few days after I got the worms, I had left them undisturbed with plenty of food and bedding, allowing them to become accustomed to their new home. They were to be a source of vermicompost to enrich the soil in my garden and would also provide an easy way to dispose of kitchen scraps in winter when outdoor compost is frozen. Even though I had been a gardener for some time and knew the value of earthworms before getting the bin, I was only aware of two types: earthworms in the garden and nightcrawlers that sprawl across the sidewalks after a soaking rain. It was at an open house at the county landfill that I first heard about composting worms. Officials were promoting consumer- and earth-friendly practices and renewing efforts to educate the public about how they could divert more waste from the landfill. Someone handed out brochures about keeping bins of composting worms. The thought of worms in the house was a little off-putting, but I was curious.

Visitors could also take a hayrack ride around the grounds for a look at where the garbage we set out each week goes. Heavy equipment lumbered around a huge pit, shifting and leveling mounds of garbage bags and other trash.

Feeding America reports that food wasted at home makes up thirty-nine percent of all food waste. Out of sight, out of mind is how we think about trash and our consumption. It's also how we think about worms, if we think about them at all. I didn't look at the worm brochure again for some time, but as I thought about how I could grow more of our own food, reduce waste, and send less to the landfill, keeping a worm bin started to make sense. We waste very little food, but I wanted to reduce our participation in the waste cycle even more if possible. For my birthday, my husband gave me a vertical bin with stackable trays, and I ordered my first batch of worms with a voucher that came with it. The vendor was in California. That summer, severe wildfires delayed shipments, and the worms were dead on arrival. I found a vendor in Wisconsin and within a couple of days had a lively bunch in hand—the ones that tried to escape.

I soon determined the worms had attempted to go over the wall because the bin was too wet. It was a common problem solved by adding a layer of shredded newspaper to absorb excess moisture. For good measure, I turned a light on above the bin so they would burrow into the bedding. When I checked an hour or so later, it appeared the worm rebellion had been quelled.

Charles Darwin long suspected that earthworms, largely dismissed by other naturalists, played a significant role in the environment. He observed them, conducted experiments, corresponded with like-minded scientists around the world, and compiled his findings in *The Formation of Vegetable Mould Through the Action of Worms with Observations on Their Habits*, published in 1881. Even though the book was dismissed by many scientists of the day, it was a seminal work. Darwin geeked out on the subject. Observing them both indoors in pots of soil and outdoors in their natural habitats, he noted what they ate, how they plugged the mouths of their burrows with different materials, how they reacted to light and vibrations, and a long list of other habits and reactions.

Worms are found all over the world except for the harshest desert and arctic regions. Oligochaetologists, those who study worms, estimate that there are about 7,000 described species, or those categorized within a taxonomy. Earthworms fall into three categories. Endogeic worms live in deep burrows and rarely come to the surface. Anecic worms, the group to which nightcrawlers belong, live in vertical burrows as deep as six feet and emerge at night to feed or to pull food back into their burrows. And finally, there are epigeic or composting worms, also called litter dwellers. They stay close to the surface living under leaves, manure piles or other decaying matter. They are not exotic; you can find them at bait shops. With a deep enough layer of decaying matter, they can live in the garden, but they are perfect for bins.

Composting worms humbly carry out their work consuming vegetable matter and bits of soil then expelling it as nutrient-rich castings. While there are several species that are good for composting, the garden variety worms we see when weeding or planting are not the same as composting worms and would not survive in a bin. *Eisenia fetida*, commonly called redworms or red wigglers, are known to be hardy and to reproduce well. These are what I have in my bin where they burrow under potato and apple peels, crushed eggshells, coffee grounds, tea bags, moldy bread and the like combined with shredded paper or cardboard and from which they create their own dark matter.

Turn over a reddish watery glob that used to be a tomato and you'll find a cluster of worms hastening its breakdown. Toss in cantaloupe rinds, and in a few days only the outermost layer remains resembling a piece of lace. When I remove the lid, the worms quickly retreat. Sometimes I can hear them moving through the lower layers. It sounds like cereal soaking up milk.

Contrary to what non-worm fanciers might think, they are neither cold nor slimy. When I drape the occasional escapee over my finger to return it to the bin, I can hardly feel it as it seems closer to the temperature of my hand. As for slime, I feel nothing on my hand even though worms do possess a small amount of mucus which allows them to burrow through decaying matter and soil.

When I put on my rubber gloves to harvest vermicompost, I spot cocoons no bigger than grains of rice nestled within the sweet-smelling crumbling matter. As much as possible, I pick them out and put them in the new bin tray among fresh scraps and paper shreds. There are also plump adults, hatchlings the size of a snippet of embroidery thread, and every size in between. The range of generations will keep the bin well populated.

It is possible for everyday bin keepers to geek out on worms, too, although maybe not in the disciplined clinical manner of Darwin. When I nudge aside that watery tomato glob, it is fun in a sort of gross way to see the pile of worms gathered under it. I'm fascinated by facts unearthed by worm scientists such as that one million earthworms in an acre of soil can create 1,200 miles of holes or burrows or, as the University of Illinois states, that 500,000 worms can create a drainage system equal to 2,000 feet of 6-inch pipe. Friends and loved ones nod and raise their eyebrows in polite amazement at such information. When a friend tosses a banana peel in the trash, I try to sound more casual than judgmental as I say, "my worms would eat that." Saving scraps leads to the occasional look of annoyance when my husband takes a container from the fridge thinking it is leftovers for reheating only to discover it's something I'm saving for the worms.

Whether in bins or gardens, lawns or farm fields, worms are unfairly demoted in our thinking. It's true they are less visible and lack the charm and beauty of butterflies, birds, and bees, but they are equally important to the ecosystem and equally vulnerable to urban development, industrial agriculture, pesticides, lawn chemicals, and other forces imposed upon them by humans. Their shy, unassuming nature and dexterous work are characteristic of their minimalist existence. They require so little yet do so much. It isn't necessary to love them, but it is necessary to sustain them.

As they consume vegetable matter and soil and burrow their way through the earth, worms expel nutrients that enable plants to resist diseases and pests. The miles of burrows they create aerate the soil enabling it to retain moisture. Tilling the garden in the spring is increasingly discouraged. It's better to leave intact the soil structure created by the worms. Last summer, my garden soil stayed moist even as dry conditions persisted. With minimal watering, the crops of tomatoes, carrots, onions, and potatoes were the best they have ever been.

Understanding the role of earthworms and their fellow organisms goes hand-in-hand with other sustainable practices that bring us into a more intimate relationship with nature. Putting one's hands to the tasks of nurturing a bin of worms, digging, planting, weeding, and watering, engages all the senses—smelling fresh earth, feeling the texture of soil, seeing worms going about their work, putting aside earbuds to hear the songs of birds, or tasting the season's first garden tomato. It rejuvenates the human spirit. It offers an alternative to passively consuming what business systems, marketing teams, and the creators of manufactured flavors place all around us.

Wendell Berry wrote, "We are working well when we use ourselves as the fellow creatures of the plants, animals, materials, and other people we are working with. Such work is unifying, healing. It… places us responsibly within the human estate."

To begin, even in a small way, to integrate ourselves into the natural systems around us by gardening in a small corner of the yard, by keeping worms in a bin, or by implementing some other practice is the most civilized thing we can do.

Gaia's Thumb
Erin Casey

Junoesque Iowa
Dennis Maulsby

The plains roll down to low-banked rivers and creeks,
flaunt weather-rounded feminine shapes.
The grassland's soft curves, like women reclining,
their graceful arms stretched overhead in naked sleep.

Breezes chuckle over their lush undulations.
Goddess faces veiled with soft green growth
make one wish to seek the red lips that must be there.
Plows of spring tattoo this earthy flesh with exotic swirls.

Female silhouettes checkered in brown or black,
jostle one another to horizon's end.
Ancient fields prepared for Nature's annual dance,
twirled to the rhapsody of wind, rain, and sun.

How the Magician King Made His Kingdom

Rachel J. Sharkey

Once upon a time, in the kingdom of Etravain, there was a prince whose mother, Alodia, had passed away. For many years, he lived alone with his father in the palace and was content. The Prince was a kind and generous man, like his father, and a clever magician, like his mother. He was widely regarded as a good heir to the kingdom. But his father, the king, was not content. When the Prince was older than a child but younger than a man, the King married a woman young enough to bear him more children.

The Prince was a kind young man who doted on his new half-siblings, but the King's second wife bore no love for her stepson and little for her new husband. Her ambition was to have her own child become king. She contrived a cunning plot to remove the Prince so her eldest son could inherit the throne in his place.

The Prince learnt of the danger he was in and had to flee into the night to escape the Queen's guards, carrying nothing but his cloak and a knife that had been his father's. His crown fell into the dirt, and he left it behind.

***

He walked through the city in despair, unsure of where to go or what to do until eventually he came to sit by his mother's grave. He sat there for a whole day and a whole night, at a loss. Eventually he could think of no better options, so at midnight, he spilt his blood upon the ground and inscribed runes into the soil to cast a spell that summoned the Ghost of his Mother's Bones.

The Ghost of his Mother's Bones arose from her grave and looked at him sadly.

"Oh my Son," she said, "what was so terrible that you felt the need to do this dreadful thing?"

The Prince laid his troubles bare before her. He had lost his birthright and lost his bloodline, and lost his home. He fell at her feet and begged her to return to him the right to his kingdom.

The Ghost of the Dead Queen Alodia listened to his woes and shook her head sadly. That was too much magic for any ghost, even the ghost of a great magician.

"Oh my Son," she said, "I cannot give you back the rights to your kingdom, for that is a claim belonging only to the line of your father. I have nothing from which I can build that can change that, for I am not strong enough. But take my burial necklace I inherited from my mother and grandmother, as a token of my bloodline, in case it can be of any help to you."

And then she faded back into the earth and the Prince could stay in the city no longer. He had stayed too long where the queen's guards would be sure to be looking for him.

***

The Prince fled into the forest in despair, unsure of where to go or what to do. His mother's necklace was cold comfort. He walked and he walked until eventually he came to the largest, oldest, and greatest tree in the very depths of the forest. He sat at the foot of the tree for two whole days and two whole nights. Eventually, he could think of no better options, so at midnight he spilt his blood upon the ground and inscribed runes into the soil to cast a spell that summoned the Ghost of the Roots of the Forest.

The Ghost of the Roots of the Forest rose from the loam.

"Oh human," she said, "what was so terrible that you felt the need to do this dreadful thing?"

The Prince laid his troubles bare before her. He had lost his birthright, and lost his bloodline, and lost his home. He fell at her feet and begged her to return to him the love of his siblings.

The Ghost of the Roots of the Forest listened to his woes and shivered her leaves.

"Oh human," she said, "I cannot return your family or build you a new one for this is not the business of trees who scatter seeds far and wide. You are welcome to become a creature of the forest and dwell among the trees. Take this cutting from my roots, which will always be a part of my family no matter where it goes, in case it is any help to you."

And then she faded back into the earth. But the Prince had grown up in cities and plains and he knew he could not thrive as a creature of the forest. The Prince stood up from the forest floor and walked away.

***

He walked towards the coast in despair, unsure of where to go or what to do. He cradled the little sapling against his chest to keep it out of the wind and sprinkled it with spring water each day. He walked and he walked until eventually he came to the base of the cliffs at the edge of the sea. Set into the cliff he found a cave leading into the depths of the Earth. The prince walked deep into the cave until he came to a crack that led down into the Earth's very heart. For three whole days and three whole nights he sat in front of the glowing heart of the Earth.. Eventually he could think of no better options, so at midnight he spilt his blood upon the ground and inscribed runes into the soil to cast a spell that summoned the ancient Ghost of the very bones of the Earth.

Slowly the ancient Ghost of the Earth emerged from the scorching chasm.

"Oh creature," she said, "what was so terrible that you felt the need to do this dreadful thing?"

And so the Prince prostrated himself before the Ghost of the Earth. He laid his troubles bare before her. He had lost his home and lost his birthright and lost his bloodline. He appealed to the Earth; to the greatest ghost that can be called, to return his home to him. The Ghost of the Earth listened to his woes. The stone she was made from shuddered and the Prince shuddered with it.

"Oh human," said the Ghost of the Earth, "all creatures are alike to me. What care I for barriers set across the ground by such small beings? What care I for how they organize themselves?"

The Prince became afraid and he cowered before the ancient Ghost of the Earth.

"Please have mercy upon me," he begged, "please accept these gifts, for the honor of your attention. They are mere trifles, but they are the entirety of my worldly wealth and as dear to me as the things I have lost."

He set before the Ghost of the Earth his father's knife, his mother's burial necklace, and the sapling child of the greatest tree in the forest.

"I need not your gifts," said the Ghost of the Earth, "and I am not unmerciful. I cannot interfere with the doings of humans, nor would I if I could, but the rising and falling of the ground is my remit entirely. If, as you say, the places you have been and the people you have loved are now inimical to you, I can create a new place for you to live and a new family to inhabit it with you."

And the Prince praised the Ghost of the Earth as both powerful and kind. Which was only correct.

The Ghost of the Earth drew heat and stone and metal from deep within herself, and from the sea, and she called up the bones of a new and clean island and clothed it with green and living things. She took the sapling child of the forest and breathed hot red motion into her cool green life to be a wife for the Prince so they could build a family together. And finally, from the Prince's blood and his mother's necklace and the metals of the island, she made the Prince a new crown. One to tie him and his children, and all the children in the line of the Dead Queen Alodia to the island for the rest of time. For the Ghost of the Earth knew more of the dealings of humans than she would admit. She left his father's knife at his feet for him to take back up. For he was a magician, like his Mother, and required a magician's tools.

***

And that is how the Exiled Prince of Etravain who was the son of the Dead Queen Alodia became the Magician King of Anara. Ever since then, Anara has been ruled by the descendants of the Magician King and his Dryad Queen. They say that if the crown were ever to change hands, the island of Anara would sink back into the sea. Let us hope we never find out if this is true.

Life of a House
Trevor Yurek

Whether in the Amazon or the local park,
they protrude and rise from the surface

These limbs of Earth grow from the soil,
protected by jagged wood like shingles on a house,
keeping what lies inside safe as best they can

Buried in the soil lies the PVC pipes of nature,
carrying currents of resources to and from the shelter above

There comes a time when a domicile is no longer suitable for residence,
no matter if the house is alive or built from parts of the dead

But homes still suitable for occupants are no safer from demolition

To the century old trees on death row; are you trembling from the wind
or the vibration of the chainsaw?

Kiln
Nicholas Lee

Metalware

J.E. Brooke

"Great gods, it actually worked."

I have no eyes to speak of, but suddenly I am aware of my surroundings and am looking down at a small woman with a large pile of brown fuzz growing out of her head. Hair, the magic provides helpfully. I should not know what any of these things are. I have never seen any of them before. I have never seen at all. But I do. The magic that woke me glows blue on her hands, the remnants beginning to fade even as the currents run up in streaks on my appendages.

Arms. Arms. Great metallic plates interconnecting until they reach my reflective carapace. I flex the sharp metal styli - fingers - of one hand, then the other, then return my awareness to the woman. I can feel the remnants of her magic when I look at her, but there is more underneath, another power that imbued me with my knowledge and purpose. It pulses when I look at this small person.

Help her, this bedrock magic whispers. She shouldn't have to grieve alone.

"Do you-" the small woman begins, but falls silent and shifts a little in front of me. She runs her hands down the thick cloth of her apron a few times, the fabric already smeared with a dusty red. I am intrigued by the color, traces of which also cling in thin, powdery crescents to the beds of her nails. An after-effect of the magic used to ignite my consciousness, perhaps? That does not seem quite right somehow, although I cannot say why. Maybe it is the difference in color. "I'm Koli," the woman says at last. "What do I call you?"

I consider a moment before answering, waiting for the magic to tell me. After the silence lengthens uncomfortably, I say, "I do not know."

"Okay," Koli says, drawing her mouth into a line and pointing the corners down. She snaps her fingers. "Can I call you Glost, at least until you decide you like something better?"

I like the way it sounds on her voice, even if I am not sure I want it to be mine forever. "Yes, Glost for now."

"Tell me when you want me to call you something else," she insists, and I nod. "Can you stand?"

Silently, I slide down from the low stone slab I had been

positioned on, planting my clawed metal feet onto the floor and rising to stand. The interlocking metal plates on my leg-appendages rasp softly as they slide against one another into their upright positions.

"How do you feel?"

Again, I am not sure how to answer. "How do I know?"

Koli's mouth makes a line again. Then she says quietly, "Does any part of you feel wrong, or out of place? Outside or in?"

"I do not think so."

"Excellent. Do you want to try walking?"

"Yes."

Koli grasps my hand as I step forward once, twice, thrice, until we have crossed the red smooth stones on the floor. The walls of the house are lined with shelves of things I cannot yet identify -- buckets of wooden and metal implements, tables draped with similarly stained cloths, and pots dripping liquid color. A hearth sits cold in the far corner of the room, behind a small table and pair of worn chairs. My steps are steady and sure, and Koli releases her grip. She opens a hole in the wall -- door -- and gestures for me to follow her through it. I step out from the house and into a riot of green, blue, and small explosions of reds, pinks, purples, yellows, and oranges. Small humming things flit between them, climbing in and out of the bells of color and then flying on to the next.

"I have something to show you," Koli says, drawing my attention back to her. The colors and sounds are almost too much, I have no reference for them, so I draw upon the small woman as an anchor. She leads me away from the overwhelming green and into a clear area at the back of the house. A fire roars red and blue in the belly of a soot-darkened metal forge. She leads me to stand in front of it, and then moves to the side, looking at me with something I think might be expectation.

"Does this call to anything in you?" Koli asks. I look at the fire, and the bent handle of the bellows. I know what these things are, what they are meant to do, but I have a suspicion that in my hands they would make nothing more than bent and twisted metal shapes, devoid of anything more. Not that I know what more would be. I do not want to meet Koli's eyes, do not want to disappoint her when she so clearly wants me to be drawn to this disused forge. I can think of nothing to say, looking around anywhere else, until I spy something else in the cleared yard next to the forge.

"What is that?" I point to the larger copy of the oven in the house. Koli's gaze follows where I indicate.

"Just my kiln," she says, eyebrows lifting.

"May I see it?"

She considers a moment. "Alright," and we walk over together.

***

Thanks to the magic driving me, once Koli says the word I know what a kiln is and what it is for even without asking her. Knowing its purpose, however, does not make the contraption less…wondrous. Impossibly, the kiln becomes moreso. My creator opens the lid and carefully removes a delicate pitcher with a long thin spout and handle styled to look like a vine. She had painted it with the liquid colors kept on the shelf inside the house, and the result is a luminous soft almost-blue green, shot through with deeper blue lines that glow and pulsate like the magic channels on my body.

"Does the magic keep them from breaking?" I ask as she places the vessel on a cart nearby, then goes back for another piece.

"Not entirely," Koli says as she works. "It strengthens the ceramic, the clay, but it can't take away the inherent weakness. Even magic can't change one thing into something else."

"Is metal alive, then?"

The ceramic witch stops mid-motion, a small cup clasped gently in her hands, and she looks from the contents of the kiln back up to me.

"No. Your skin is metal, but you, Glost, you're something special. Something new. The work of a lifetime, you might say, or several. And it's up to you to figure out exactly what that means."

"You cannot tell me?"

Koli laughs, and something in my components warms. I am not sure what that means.

"Unfortunately, I can't. That was one part of living that we couldn't change, among others." Her mouth still curves up in a smile, but it takes on an odd twist I have not seen from her that does not seem to fit the cheerful sound of her voice. I am not sure what that means, either, but I want to figure it out. She finishes loading the cart, answering my questions – although I do not ask about the strange not-smile. Calling attention to it does feel wrong, like something wrenched and twisted out of place as Koli said. At least for now. Later, the magic whispers softly. For now, I help her take the cart back into the house when she asks.

***

Early the next morning, I load the pieces into the back of a wagon as Koli tells me what route I am supposed to take to reach town.

"You are not coming?"

Her mouth does the not-quite-smile again. "I – no. Not this time, at least. I know you can do this, Glost. You'll be alright and I'll be here when you come back. If you have any questions, the other vendors know me, and they'll help you if you tell them you're there on my behalf."

"Very well," I say, still feeling that wrongness about asking why she does not want to go. "What will you do?"

"I have some pieces to construct and let harden, and the kiln needs to be stoked before I can fire the leather-hard pieces on the worktable. I'll be alright, Glost, and so will you."

"Very well," I say but somehow know we will revisit this later. She helps me gain a strong grip on the handles of the cart, tucks a map in amongst the carefully wrapped wares in case I lose my way, and wishes me a safe journey as I begin walking toward town.

***

The road at first is lined with deep rows of trees, their branches and leaves spreading over the road to shelter its travelers. Sunlight dapples down through the leaves. I cannot feel it on my carapace, but I imagine it is quite pleasant to other creatures. I can just hear them rustling under the brown leaves carpeting the ground under the bows and branches.

Eventually, I come upon more houses set among the trees. I see more people, but they remain in their houses, watching me from the cracks of shuttered windows. They do not smile at my approach. I do not think much of it, I have work that needs to be done. I promised Koli that it would be, and I do not want to let her down.

In front of another house, there is a small human. Smaller than any I have seen so far. As I approach, she is concentrating fiercely on knocking perfectly round, smooth stones into one another within a circle of rope arranged on the ground. She hears me as I pass by though, and looks up to watch me. She stands, and I half expect her to run into the house with the other humans. She does not. The small human sprints with impressive speed through the gate and out into the road, up to me.

"Delv? Is that you?"

"I am sorry," I reply. "I do not know who that is. My name is Glost."

She considers me a moment, then plants her feet apart a bit more and says, "You're big like Delv, but I guess you don't look like him. I like your blue ribbons; they're pretty. I'm Adne. Bye!" And before I can say anything else she shoots back into the yard and over to her game. I stand in the road, perplexed by the small human's erratic behavior, but I cannot linger long. Koli is depending on me to sell her vessels. The momentary confusion breaks, and I continue on.

The market down the road is full of humans, and they part for me as I walk up the road into their midst. The loud collective murmur dies quickly as they see me, and for a moment we simply look at each other. I pause for the magic to inform me of what to do next, but it stays frustratingly silent on how to interact with these new humans. Koli tried to prepare me, though. "Koli sent me. My name is Glost," I say exactly as we practiced earlier. Then, remembering my interaction with Adne, I add, "I am not Delv."

Someone in the crowd laughs but cuts it off sharply. A few people step forward, their mouths twisting up like Koli's does when she is pleased with something. "Welcome, Glost," one of them says and holds their hand out to me. I am not sure what they want me to do with it. "We can show you where Koli has her stall."

The cart is significantly lighter and emptier by the time I begin down the road to return to Koli's house. Home, the magic supplies, and I register frustration -- which is new -- at its strange timing. Why could it not have returned earlier to tell me what to do around these other humans? I hope it will not abandon me with Koli as well. Thankfully, she set the prices and some of the other vendors helped me navigate interactions with customers who wanted to haggle too low. I do not like haggling, too many questions that I do not know how to answer. Fortunately, the helpful vendors seemed to know the minimum price Koli would accept. I plan to ask her more about this later, so that next time I can be better. The metal box with bronze, silver, and gold chits rattles around inside my carapace where I have stored it for safekeeping on the road. The sun is setting by the time I pass Adne's house, and the small human is no longer in the yard. Her house is still shuttered, but now a warm flicker of yellow-orange light leaks through the cracks in the boards. Will there be similar light coming from Koli's house when I return? I hope so.

***

There is no light coming from the house when I pass into the main yard. The kiln smokes, though, and I can see that the shelves of waiting pieces are less crowded than it was when I left. I do not find Koli at first, until I hear a small sound that reminds me of the noise from an unenchanted pot that fell from a nearby table at the market onto cobbles. The sound is still distinctly Koli, and I leave the cart to follow it to a thick copse of trees and flowers hidden between the kiln and the forge. The clay witch is draped over a large, perfectly flat stone set into the ground. The inlaid metal in the stone glows blue in the dying light, illuminating Koli's heaving breaths as she makes another shattered sound. A sharp feeling of displacement slashes through me – fear, says the magic – and I am already moving toward her by the time I am aware of it.

"Koli?" I ask to gain her attention more than anything, my voice doing strange things without permission. The woman turns, though, and looks at me.

"Glost," Koli says, her face puffed, red, and wet. Is she sick? "I'm sorry, I must have lost track of time." She wipes at her cheeks as she stands, and then runs her damp hands down her clay-stained apron in turn. "How was the market? I'll help you with the cart." She moves from the stone toward the path back to the yard, nearly matching Adne's speed. I turn to follow, but as I revolve away from the stone I see a name illuminated by the glowing metal magic.

Delv.

***

After we finish emptying the cart, Koli lights the lamps and I follow her instructions to light a fire in the hearth. There are several new pieces shaped out of still-wet clay that were not on the table this morning when I left. I examine each without touching them, repeating the names of their forms in my head as my sharp fingers ghost over each one. Cup, vase, saucer, ewer. Lines have been scored in them already, to be filled with magic later Koli said. There is a curious buzzing beneath the metal of my fingers. I do not think it is a malfunction, but it is not something I am able to ignore. I follow the buzzing with my hand to lift the delicate oil ewer that has been left to dry.

"What are you doing, Glost?" Koli asks, catching me completely unaware. Her voice is gentle but the shock I get from its sudden intrusion sends a shudder through me, making my fingers seize and then reflexively close. The sharp points of the digits slice clean through the soft material of the unfinished vessel. Everything stops. Koli goes still, and I am filled with a sudden sense of wrongness that I myself am the source of. I have broken something beautiful without meaning to, and the horror of it sends me reeling backwards, dropping the severed hunks of clay back onto the table in misshapen lumps. "Glost," Koli says in a small voice that sends me flying from the room.

Last night, before she went to sleep, Koli had taken me to a different room and showed me a large bed piled with soft things. "It's yours," she said, and then walked on to her own room. I did not need to sleep, I am not sure if I ever will, so instead of confining myself I went back out into the yard as quietly as I was able and spent the night examining and trying to understand what Koli and the magic referred to as stars. I still do not need to sleep, but after breaking the soft-clay piece I want to burrow myself away somewhere and so I find the room that Koli said was mine, sit on the bed and draw some of the blankets tightly over myself. I try to do it all carefully, not wanting to break anything else with my sharp fingers. Why were they made so sharp? The tight pressure of the blankets around me is soothing, and I begin to calm a little, the wanting-to-fly-away feeling receding just as Koli comes into the space.

"Glost, are you alright?" There is a creak and depression in the mattress as she sits down beside me.

"I am sorry," I say, something restricting my voice and making it small. "I broke the beautiful thing."

"I can make it again," Koli says gently. "I'm not angry or upset," she offers, and it does make me feel better to hear. "I was worried about you. You picked it up to get a better look at it, didn't you?"

"Yes," I admit. I pull one of the blankets off so that I can see her. I hold up one of my sharp hands as well and say, "There was. A buzzing, in my fingers. I do not know how else to describe it. It felt right to touch."

Koli smiles, a real smile now, and makes a show of wrapping her hand around my own. "Would you like to learn how I make them?"

***

The next market is not for several days, so the first thing we do the next morning is go out to the forge where she helps me start the grindstone spinning. A shower of sparks later, and my fingers are less sharp, less likely to damage.

"We – it was hard to know what you would need to be able to grip," Koli says after apologizing to me again as I smooth down any remaining rough edges of the digits on the buffing wheel. "Does that hurt?"

I pull the last of my fingers away, assessing their suitability. They look less like claws and more like Koli's now. There is no wrong-feeling in them, what I think she would call pain.

"No, it does not feel like anything."

"Okay. Then let's go back inside and get started."

We sit down at the canvas-covered work table, already smeared with the faded stains of old projects. Or, I try to sit down. The other stool she has pulled up to the workspace is too tall, and I hang over the table, arms struggling to reach any meaningful closeness, the joints of my legs banging against the underside of the lip. I try to adjust, but Koli sees my struggle anyway and runs out of the room for a moment. She returns with a shorter seat for me to try, and it is an enormous improvement. She cuts hunks of clay from a larger slab that she covers with waxed cloth before returning to the table. There is a strange gleam in Koli's eyes that I have not seen before, though I know that does not mean very much. She is not smiling but, somehow, this is the happiest she has been since I've known her. She moves with purpose, not a gesture or a step wasted as she amasses clay and tools and comes back to the table with full arms.

For a while, we just sit and work our respective clay hunks between our fingers. "To get a feel for it," Koli says but gives no further instructions. So we sit, and I adjust my digits into being tools. They are awkward at first, even with the points gone, but the more I mold the clay into random shapes the more familiar and comfortable the movements and material feel. I wonder if the rest of living will be this way.

***

The next market day, Koli sends me alone again to sell her cart full of wares in the busy square. She lingers in the yard, waving as I go in the soft dawn light. Adne is not in her yard this time as I pass, and I register an odd hollowness in my carapace at the lack of the small human. I wanted to see her again. I am past the house and leaving its view as I hear a low thunk from behind. Thinking to protect Koli's work, I wheel around in time to see the door to the house swing shut again behind a rapidly advancing blur.

"Glost!" Adne shouts, bursting through the gate and running up to me. "I hoped you'd be back!" She reaches up and holds out a small white flower. "Yours," she says. Carefully, I pinch the stem between my fingers and keep it there, awkwardly. I cannot pull the cart and hold the flower at the same time, so I slip the stem into the space between two segments on the upper part of my arm.

"Thank you," I say.

"'Kay, Glost. Bye!" Adne grins wildly and then dashes back through the gate.

I look down at the flower, swaying a little from its new perch as I resume walking down the path. I keep it there during the market, which seems to amuse some of the other vendors and the customers. I am beginning to recognize some of them from the first time, which pleases me. I require less help from the other vendors this time figuring how to set up the pieces and count back chits, but they are still friendly and ask to make sure I do not need anything else. They ask after Koli, and I do not know how to respond. They do not mention Delv, but I think that they want to. We pack up our things at the end of the day and leave the square together. I tower over the five others scattered around me, and I move slowly as we walk not wanting to hurt them. But they move easily, loosely around me with their carts. They talk and laugh around me and in a few moments we part to go our separate ways, wishing each other well until the next market.

***

It is almost dark again by the time I reach home. Koli is in the yard again instead of bent over the stone in the glen. Her apron is stained with red streaks that weren't there earlier this morning, so I know that she has moved since this morning. But her eyes are read and puffed like they were the last time I came home. I wish she did not try to hide this feeling that causes her so much pain. I want to help her, but I do not know how. And the magic will not tell me, no matter how much I ask it. As I learn more about this life and this world that I inhabit, the voice becomes less frequent and more selective about what it will tell me. On matters of human emotion, it is basically silent except for when it urges me again to "Help Koli." I am doing my best, but sometimes I worry that I am failing us all.

We move on from playing with clay to something Koli calls "slab work". She helps me line up smooth wooden sticks to frame and roll out sheets of clay that we cut, score along the edges, and leave to dry leather-hard. Then we take watery clay (slip, she calls it, and it is by far the most accurate name of anything I have yet come across) and brush the raised score marks to get the pieces to stick together. I look down at the small gray box that I have created, unimpressed. It seems so plain – dull, next to the things that I have seen the witch create.

She must sense my disappointment. "It's good work," she says, lightly touching my arm. "You've learned a lot already."

"Thank you for teaching me. Will you show me how to make the magic lines like your works have?"

"When it's dry. But we've done enough for the day. Come, I have a new story for you tonight." We pass the rest of the evening by the fire, Koli reading from her newest book until she yawns and dismisses herself to bed.

The next day the edges have dried enough so that we can etch thin lines into the surface of the sides. At first, I try to imitate her designs but my fingers itch until I allow them to take over. The result looks nothing like Koli's, but I like them all the same. I look down to her, only to see her smiling back up at me. Her fingers glow blue, and she touches one of the lines. Blue light floods into the piece, filling each one until the whole piece is saturated. "Here," she says, turning towards me, "I'll do yours..."

But I have already willed some of the blue glow into my own fingers, touching one to the line like I watched her do a moment ago.

"Glost! Are you alright?"

"Yes?" I reply, pulling my hands back. The glow fades from my hands as my concentration breaks in the confusion. "What did I do wrong?" She takes one of my hands in hers and turns it over gently.

"Nothing," she murmurs. "It's all still there. I was worried you'd use up your magic, but it's – you haven't lost any of it." She looks back down to the small blue-tinged box still glowing on the table. "Glost, you're amazing."

I do not know how to answer, but behind my carapace something within me glows warm.

We fire the pieces at the end of the week, after coating them in dull glaze. "The colors will be brighter after they're fired," Koli promises before they go in. When the kiln is cool enough again, we open the lid to utter devastation.

"Oh Glost, I'm sorry," Koli says as she pulls shards of sky-blue almost-box from among the other intact pieces. "There must have been an air bubble. It happens sometimes, but that doesn't make it any less sad. It would have been beautiful."

"Can we try it again?" I ask, admiring the piece of sky in my hand.

"Of course we can."

***

We do. The next piece I make, an almost identical box also painted with sky blue glaze, comes out of the kiln intact, and is placed on the highest shelf in my room, where I can look at it on my shelf. Someone created me, and now I have created something in turn with Koli's guidance. I cannot smile, but I feel the now familiar warmth in my carapace that I think must mean that I would if I could. I begin another slab piece, and while we wait for that to dry, Koli teaches me how to use the pottery wheel. The first attempt ends up a splatter on the wall because I move the pedal too fast in my eagerness. The clay witch laughs as we clean up and begin again, and this time I am more restrained. The resulting shape is not what I think could be called anything, really, but it is still satisfying even as I crumple it into a ball to begin the piece again.

***

The days grow longer. I leave for the market a little earlier each week, but without fail Adne is there to greet me as I pass her house, often not alone. Sometimes she's joined by larger, older members of her family, but more often she's joined by a steadily growing group of other small humans who all cry out in delight as I come into view and run to keep up with me for a short way down the road. The white flowers are gone now, but the small humans find more blossoms in an impressive array of colors. I accept each one as gently as I can and tuck the blooms in the gaps between the plates on my arms. I am a walking garden by the time I reach the market. Sometimes bees and butterflies land to sip nectar and collect pollen. The market folk still stare at me in wonder, but they are friendly now for having gotten to know me, and I am friendly with them in turn. They always ask after Koli, but now they are more open in their curiosity about me, and more open about the fact that they miss Delv.

Delv, I learn, was Koli's person for many years. Until he became sick. I don't understand at first, so one of my friends from the market explains. "It's when – when you don't function properly," Liri, a glassblower from a nearby stall, says quietly while we are packing up our stalls for the week. "And sometimes you stop functioning altogether and just cease."

I try to imagine it, not being, again. I remember becoming myself, but nothing of what came before, what might come after. "And that's what happened to Delv?" Liri nods, eyes suddenly shining.

"We haven't seen Koli since. She just shut herself away. We're worried about her, and we miss her. Then, you started coming to the market, and now I think she's coming back to herself."

"What do I have to do with any of this?"

"You're helping her create again."

"Is that my purpose then?"

"Your purpose is to be, my dear." Liri pats my arm. "The same as any other person. We find healing in each other, more often than not. That's how you're helping her now. And if you ever need it, there are other people who will be able to help you."

***

I think about what Liri said the whole walk back home. I must approach more quietly than usual, or else the lengthening days must play with Koli's sense of time because she isn't in the yard when I arrive with an empty cart. I find her in the glen for the first time in months. She's not bent over Delv's stone this time, but sitting beside it. Her cheeks are wet again, but she's not sobbing the way she had been the last time. I approach carefully, slowly, not wanting to startle her. The magic pulses, urging me to go on, but I don't need to be told now. I want to help because, I hope, I can. Because, if Liri is to be believed, I already am.

"Hello Glost," Koli said softly, looking up at me from Delv's grave. "How was the market?"

"It went well," I say, coming over to where she's sitting. I sit down beside her on the long summer grass and pull my clicking legs in close. The sun is going down and the light is stained orange with purple shadows. "Liri says hello."

"Oh, how is Liri?" Koli says, smiling but not moving to stand.

"She seems well," I say, and then, carefully, add, "She misses you."

A fat tear rolls down Koli's cheek as she looks back to Delv's stone. She sighs heavily and leans into me. I lock the joints in my arms to support her. We sit quietly like that until the light is almost gone except for the blue magic light of the gravestone and the distant specks of stars. "I miss her too," she says at last. "I miss them all."

"Will you tell me about him?" I ask. "Delv? Your person?"

That wins a quiet laugh mixed with a sob, but Koli says, "Maybe it's time that I did."

"Delv was your person, wasn't he?"

Koli nods. "He was. He was my favorite person. We made a life together, learned to make magic together. He was the most gifted metallurgist I'd ever met, even without his magic. I'm sure by now you've guessed the forge was his. That's where he built your carapace. He'd started working on it before he got sick, and he knew you'd be his last work. His greatest work. I contributed some ceramic components, and we both added our magic. His own first, and then, after he was gone, I added my own to wake you. No one had done anything like it before, I'm not sure anyone will again. I'm so glad you're here with me, Glost."

"I'm glad to be with you here," I reply softly. The magic swirls blue up my arms and I make a decision. "I think - I think that Delv speaks to me. Sometimes. Through the magic. He's tried to help us both, right from the very beginning." Koli is shaking now, gripping my arm, but I can see her smile as the tears flow and drip into the grass. "Come with me to the market, next time. You have people who care about you there too."

"I think I'd like that, Glost," Koli says shakily, but there is resolve beneath the tremor in her voice. My carapace warms.

***

The next market day, we load the cart full of our wares and start down the road together.

***

Flat Earth
R. R. Brown

High school teacher Joe Leonard slouches in his chair and stares at the clock. On his desk lay a folder containing the lesson plan imposed upon him by the School Board. He taps the folder and sighs. In just ten minutes, he'll have to present this course to his freshman geography class. He's dreading it. In fact, he briefly considered walking down to the office and telling the vice-principal that he'd eaten something bad for lunch and needed to go home, but he just couldn't bring himself to do it. His students would know he'd chickened-out and he simply couldn't have that. So, with time running out, he keeps searching for a way to do the Boards' bidding without losing his soul in the process.

How did it come to this sad state of affairs? One year ago, the U.S. Supreme Court, led by its conservative originalists, took the vote away from anyone who didn't have a deed to property. The decision effectively destroyed the Democratic Party. While much of the nation convulsed in violent protest, the citizens of Joe's school district in rural Iowa didn't make much of a fuss. The students conducted walk-out protests during the two weeks following the Court's decision, but the demonstrations ended when their parents, fearful of community backlash, threatened to take away their car keys and mobile phones if they didn't go back to their classes.

A few months after the Court's decision, the district's propertied class voted to replace the old School Board members with Christians committed to traditional moral values, the kind of values described in the Bible, the kind that would, in the words of the new Board President, "… curb the base and destructive instincts we see in our children." The new Board wasted no time in acting. The library, teacher resources, and school curriculum were scrubbed of anything that did not reflect Christian beliefs. Motivational posters and art were replaced with framed Bible quotes and the school's Intranet was configured to block access to anything that didn't fit the new moral framework.

Teachers, stunned by the Court's decision and shell-shocked from watching months of televised rioting, were devastated by the Board's looting of their offices and libraries. They stumble about the school like zombies with the school's universal textbook, the New International version of the Bible, tucked under their arms.

Joe Leonard had hoped to avoid the anti-secular activities of the School Board. After all, geography is the study of the Earth's topography, its climate, population, and land use. It could hardly be thought of as a topic of moral interest to Christians. And for a while, he continued to teach geography in the way he'd always done it. His class, free of the religious doctrine that permeated all their other classes, became popular with his students. In fact, he's never had a class so interested in geography.

Then came the night when the School Board's President proposed that flat-earth principles be used as the basis for the high school geography class. Joe, who was present at the meeting, stood up to tell the Board that the shape of the Earth is settled science. The President shot back, "Nowhere in the Bible does it say the Earth is shaped like a basketball." She called for a vote, which was carried unanimously.

The next day, all of the round desk globes were taken to the landfill, along with any text books and wall maps that illustrated or described the Earth as spherical. Deprived of the tools of his trade, Joe's class temporarily became a study hall while he waited for the Board to procure new course materials. He got them yesterday, right at the end of the school day. He read them over dinner, which spoiled a perfectly good casserole. While he and his wife tidied up from their meal and on through the rest of the evening's activities, they argued about Joe quitting his job, but he was only two years away from retirement and the lucrative pension he'd earned from a life-time of public service. The President of the Board had him by the balls and there was nothing he could do about it, except toss and turn through the night.

The numerals on the classroom clock blur from Joe's staring at them. He blinks them clear and sees there's now only five minutes before the bell that will call the students to his classroom. Among the students will be the Board President's daughter, Sydney, the teenage Bible expert and the prettiest girl in the school. She roams the halls surrounded by her attendants, holding court like a queen. Sydney is also her mother's eyes and ears within the school.

Also in the class will be the school's star basketball player, Aaron, whose father was one of the original founders of a large tech company. When Aaron was ten years old, his family bought 40-acres in the school district so his mom could operate a small farm to raise hormone and antibiotic free food for the family. Shortly after they moved in, his father made a big splash by donating the millions needed to build a new athletic complex for the school.

Aaron's father is one of the few propertied Democrats in a poor school district overwhelmingly controlled by Republicans. His power is his wealth. After the Board turned itself into the school's Elders, he withdrew his promise of funding for a new library and began attending every Board meeting where he delighted in tormenting Sydney's mother. Like father, like son, Aaron has been the radical voice of secularism within the student body. He and Sydney have clashed at every turn, just like Aaron's father and Sydney's mother, but unlike their parents, there's the promise of a tragedy because it's plain to Joe that underneath all their animosity, there's good chemistry.

The bell rings and the hall fills with the sound of students on the move. Resigned to his fate, Joe wakes the computer and launches the presentation, then buries his face in his hands while he waits for the program to load.

When the Board voted to revise Joe's curriculum, tension began building throughout the school. Everyone knew that Joe's geography class was the last vestige of the "old" school, even the math class had begun calculating everything in palms, spans and cubits. On the day Joe would teach his students that the Earth is flat, secularism would have taken its last breath.

Joe hadn't said anything to anyone about getting his new course materials, but word leaked nonetheless. Text messages flew about that evening while Joe and his wife argued over what to do. When his students filed into the classroom, they did so quietly, including Sydney, who checked her glee when she saw Joe's face in his hands. They took their seats and, out of respect for the school's most senior teacher, they kept their voices to a whisper.

Joe had been dreaming of his days as a young man in the Navy when he realized he'd fallen asleep. He raises his head from his hands and sees the students in their seats looking toward him, wide-eyed in anticipation, with the exception of Sydney, who's spoiling for a fight, and Aaron, who's ready to give her one.

Joe sits up and clears his throat. "I'm sorry," he mumbles. "I didn't sleep very well last night."

He reaches for his cup of coffee, grown cold during his brief nap, and swallows a mouth-full of the sour brew, then rubs his eyes until they're pink.

"Alright," he says, brightening. "Let's get after it." He turns on the projector and the screen fills with a large circular map. Above the map, in bold block letters, is the title: The Earth is Flat. Marked in the center of the map is the North Pole. Surrounding the pole are five continents: The Americas, Australia, Asia, Europe and Africa.

Joe gets up from his desk and regards the map. "Notice anything unusual?" he asks his students.

Josie, his brightest student, points out that the continent of Antarctica is missing.

Joe picks up a pointer and traces the thin, white strip that surrounds the outside of the circular map. "It's here," he says. "It's the ice wall that goes around the outside of the Earth. It prevents the ocean's waters from spilling over the edge and into the void."

Aaron snorts. "Oh, yes," he chortles. "And I'm Taylor Swift!"

"You got a problem?" Sydney snaps over nervous laughter.

Aaron screws up his face in disgust, but before he can respond, Bradley, a quiet boy who rarely participates, chimes in. "I see the equator is still in the same place. If you travel the equator through the continents, is it still, what, 25,000 miles, right?"

"That's right," Joe answers. "We learned that earlier in the semester."

Casey, the resident math expert, holds up a hand. Joe recognizes him. "Okay, the equator is halfway between the North Pole and the ice wall, which makes the ice wall double the distance of the equator, or about 50,000 miles…"

"Huh," Aaron deadpans.

"…which," Casey continues, ignoring Aaron's comment, "would make the Earth twice as big as it's currently thought to be."

"Whoa…" Aaron says in mock astonishment. "Really?"

"Where's the South Pole?"

Joe searches for the unfamiliar voice. It's Avery, the goth girl that sits in the back row. She's always attentive and she does well on her homework and tests, but this is the first time she's felt the need to ask a question.

"Well," Joe explains, "the word "pole" in the context of the Earth would normally mean the end of an axis through a spherical body, but in flat-Earth theory…"

Sydney loudly clears her throat.

"… but here," he amends, correcting himself, "the Earth is a flat, circular world, not a sphere. No sphere, no axis. No axis, no poles."

"But, there is a North Pole," Avery presses. "It's right there on the map."

Joe shrugs.

Sydney can't keep quiet any longer. "It got its name from people who misunderstood the true shape of the Earth."

There's a collective groan from the class and Sydney's cheeks color.

Casey jumps back in. "So, you're suggesting that if everyone in the world headed south, they wouldn't meet at the same place, but end up spread out along 50,000 miles of ice wall?"

"That's what the map suggests," Joe answers, careful to distinguish the lesson from his personal beliefs.

"That doesn't make any sense," Avery concludes, sitting back and folding her arms.

Joe spies Sydney. Her face has darkened. He takes a different tack.

"Actually, our senses are at the heart of flat-Earth theory," he explains.

"It's not a theory," Sydney snarls, but Joe continues as if he hasn't heard her.

"Look out the window. The ground looks pretty flat, doesn't it?"

One of the students says "Welcome to Iowa," and the class laughs at the old joke.

"And the clouds look pretty flat along their bottoms, too," he points out. The class grows nervous, uncertain as to where Joe is going. Is he arguing for a flat Earth? Even Sydney isn't sure.

"Seeing is believing, isn't it?" Joe asks.

Sydney makes a noise of agreement and visibly relaxes.

"What the astronauts saw doesn't count?" Casey asks, tugging on his Snoopy in Space t-shirt.

"What astronauts?" Sydney asks.

Joe quickly steps in before Aaron can say anything. "People who subscribe to a flat Earth say no one's ever left the Earth's atmosphere and claims of people in space are just the government's attempt to break down people's beliefs and make them susceptible to government manipulation."

"But there are pictures!" Casey persists, "The big, blue marble!"

"Fake," Sydney counters. "The pictures were faked. Easy to do. I mean, seriously. Walking on the moon? How ridiculous. Do any of you personally know anyone who's been to outer space?"

The class stares at her.

"Seeing is believing, that's all I'm trying to say."

"You mean," Aaron says, leaning toward Sydney, "believing is seeing. Right? Seeing what fits your beliefs and ignoring everything that doesn't?"

Aaron's comment gives Joe an opportunity to talk about something he wouldn't have dared to do on his own. He steps into a row and spreads his arms. "We can't personally experience everything there is to know. There's just too much of it. It's logical to depend on others for the knowledge we don't have, like Jason over at the garage who takes care of our brakes, or Jayne and Ella at the clinic who see us when we're sick." Joe pauses, nodding in Sydney's direction, "How can we trust them to take care of us?"

Sydney opens her mouth, but hesitates.

"Go on," Joe encourages.

"Because our parents and friends said we can trust them." Sydney answers.

"And when we have to deal with people outside our community, how can we know we can trust them?"

Joe sees Sydney's thinking and holds up a hand to give her time to think. Finally, she says, "We have to rely on our senses."

"Alright," Joe replies. "Let's talk about our senses. They're powerful. They do a great job of helping us interpret the world around us, but sometimes we get confused by them. Has anyone seen what happens when you put a stick in water?"

Several in the class nod.

"A straight stick appears to bend, right?"

More nods.

"And when we pull it out, the stick is straight again. We saw it with our own eyes, but does that mean the stick bends when it goes in the water?"

"No," Josie answers, pushing her glasses up the bridge of her nose. "The stick looks like it bends because water is more dense than air. There's a name for it, but I can't remember what it's called."

"Reflection," Brady offers. He's the biggest kid in the class and normally a jokester. Everyone looks at him. "What?" he asks, throwing up his palms.

"You're close," Joe says. "It's called refraction. Our eyes see the difference in how light travels in water and air as a bent stick, but since we don't understand what's actually happening, we think our eyes are tricking us. We want to rely on our senses, but sometimes what our senses are trying to tell us doesn't fit with what we believe, so we ignore them. Even our friends who believe in a flat Earth will tell you that a ship disappearing over the horizon is a trick of the eye."

Sydney scowls, but says nothing.

Joe walks toward the front of the room and gazes up at the map of the flat Earth. "We go through our days without having to think too much about what's happening around us, but sometimes we see or hear something that doesn't fit with what we believe to be true. If it's our senses telling us, we might say 'my eyes are tricking me' or 'I'm hearing things' and move on without another thought." He points up at the map of the flat Earth. "But what if it's another person who tries to convince us of something that doesn't fit with our beliefs?"

He glances over his shoulder at the class.

"Our first reaction is to defend what we believe to be true, like Casey did when he talked about the pictures of the Earth from outer space. But that didn't change Sydney's mind, nor anyone else who believes that the Earth is flat. So, the next thing that we do is to try and poke holes in the other person's belief, as Avery did when she pointed out that there's no South Pole. But even that wasn't enough to change Sydney's mind, was it?"

Sydney shakes her head.

"So," Joe says, folding his arms, "when both sides are at an impasse and when neither side is willing to budge, what do you think will happen next?"

No one seems willing to venture a guess, so Joe tells them. "Things get personal. We accuse each other of being stupid or ignorant. If the situation isn't defused, someone will stomp off or end up taking a swing at the other person. And, as we've seen in matters of religion throughout history, we might even try to kill each other."

Joe looks down at the lesson plan on his desk. He could hear a pin drop in the class. He sighs, picks up the lesson, and turns back to the class.

"Fortunately, there's another way," he says, waving the lesson plan. "Instead of arguing or fighting, we could take the time to understand - truly understand - what the other person is trying to tell us."

Joe points to his temples. "We can listen to what they have to say with an open mind. If it turns out that what the other person is saying has merit, it just might change our minds about a few things. But if, after careful consideration, what they're saying doesn't move you, well, you've simply gained more confidence in the beliefs you already had."

Joe sits back on his desk. "It's kind of a win-win thing, don't you think?"

The kids look at each other.

Aaron's face scrunches in disbelief. "You want us to try and prove the Earth is flat?"

"No, not that," Joe clarifies. "Just give their argument some serious thought. Examine the evidence for a flat Earth that we can all agree on, what we call objective evidence, and set aside anything that we can't agree on. Be sensitive to folks who are skeptical of "expert" opinion. If you want to bring evidence that you haven't personally experienced, be prepared to explain why the source can be trusted."

Joe sees several students writing in their notepads. "And when you're done, compare what you've found to what you already know. Think about it like a pendulum scale, stacking the objective evidence for a flat Earth on one side and objective evidence for a spherical Earth on the other."

One of the kids asks for an example of objective evidence. Joe points to the front of the class. "I think we can all agree on the color of the white board."

"Oh!" Aaron moans, "You gave it away!"

The student's laugh. Even Sydney laughs.

"And Sydney," Joe continues, "Can you do the same for a spherical planet? Look at the evidence and compare it to what you know? Can you do that for us?"

Sydney rubs at something on her desktop, then relents. "Alright," she says, her forehead tied in a little knot.

"Is there anyone else who wants to look at the evidence for a spherical world?"

Sydney has been such a giant pain in the ass lately that Joe doesn't expect anyone to volunteer, but then he sees Josie, his star student, raise her hand.

"I'll work with her," Josie volunteers, then twists in her chair to look at Sydney. "Honestly, Syd, I've always taken a spherical world for granted. I need to look into it for my own good!"

"I'll go with them!" Avery volunteers, tossing her head to flip the hair from her eyes.

"Me, too," says the boy sitting next to Avery, who has been sneaking sidelong looks at her.

"Very good," Joe concludes. He looks up at the clock and catches Aaron's hand out of the corner of his eye.

"Yes, Aaron."

"I'd like to be on Sydney's team, too."

"Whoa…," says Jonah, a fellow basketball player who sits behind Aaron.

"Very good," Joe says. "Casey, can you take the lead for those who will offer objective evidence for a flat Earth?"

His math expert accepts without hesitation.

Joe turns to the white board and makes two lists, one for those researching the evidence for a flat planet and those researching the evidence for a spherical planet, then gives final instructions.

"Do your research at home," he suggests, mindful of the restrictions placed on the school's intranet. "Remember, it's not a debate and it's not a contest. The assignment is about looking critically at new ideas and challenging your own assumptions."

He puts the marker in the tray and walks back to his desk. "It's about learning to think for yourself and each of you will make your own decision as to which idea is the most compelling to you."

Joe goes back to sitting on the edge of his desk. "And no matter what decision you come to, everyone in the class will respect you, because you took the time to truly understand the evidence before you. Are there any questions?"

The bell rings in answer and the students rise to gather their things. Joe walks around his desk and sinks into his chair. He's relieved that class is over, but more than that, he's humbled by how the kids handled the subject. In fact, in all his years of teaching, has he ever had a better experience in a classroom? He shakes his head, smiles, and takes a sip of his coffee. Its bitter taste makes him wince.

When he looks up, he sees Sydney standing by the door, holding her backpack against her chest. She's looking at him with a thoughtful expression. When he meets her gaze, she nods and heads out the door. Joe watches her go.

He'd lost hope over the past year - hope for the country, for his school, and for the future of his students, but after today's class…. Well, thanks to his kids, he's found a way to fight back. For a moment, he thinks his emotions might get the best of him, but the feeling passes. He reaches for his coffee cup and just as he's bringing it to his lips, he remembers its awful taste and sets it down. He turns off the projector, puts the computer to sleep, and heads for the teacher's lounge.

The End

Your Roots are Showing
Spike Dawkins

Some Dirt
Mike Keller-Wilson

Don't be a pansy, he said. Rub some dirt on it and get back into left field.

So that's what I did, scooped up some dusty clay and the smashed husk of a withered acorn and left Father/Coach behind.

The dirt was stinging the gash up my leg before I stopped to think that Father/Coach may not have said exactly what he meant. But then, the next batter was approaching the plate, and Coach—just Coach, now—was yelling at us to shift left and watch the baseline goddammit.

I was thinking about the first time I hit off a tee. It had been a piddly little smack that knocked the ball into the dirt where a pitcher would normally stand. It was enough for a homerun, at least in tee ball. Back then, I'd heard the glimmer of a long-dead hope come alive in my father's cheering voice as I crossed home plate. The same hope had thrummed in his arms as he lifted me onto his shoulders. When was the last time I'd felt like that, hefted above the weight of his expectations?

Still, I tried to shift left, to watch the baseline. Even with the stinging up my leg and behind my eyes, I really tried. It was no use. I'd settled back onto my heels; it was as if my cleats had taken root now that they'd finally found nurturing soil.

The ballfield was well-tended—cared for by the city's head groundskeeper, a man with calloused hands who made sure to visit the field after particularly hard rains to ensure proper drainage. He did this, even on his days off, for two reasons: his only son, grown now, had played ball there and it made him think of that Field of Dreams movie. They'd watched it together a handful of times when his son still played. Now, the two fields were linked somewhere in the deep roots of his mind.

This groundskeeper was the man the city called when an oak tree took root and sprouted to a five-meter height between batters at a youth game one Saturday. They didn't mention the oddly-timed disappearance of the left fielder in that game. That story would come to dominate the regional news before long: endless clips of a bereft father only just realizing what he'd lost. When the groundskeeper arrived, he found what looked to be a nine-year-old red oak that he couldn't bring himself to cut down. Instead, he made plans for rotating the field so the tree would be beyond the fence line. Finally, he used an extendable pruning saw to retrieve the mitt from the end of a tree limb in the crown, as if it had been expecting a fly ball.

They Buried Me on Sunday
Erin Casey

They buried me on Sunday
because I'd learned the truth.
They thought that they could silence me,
but my death became the proof.

***

Let's start at the beginning
in a village of great renown.
My name's Eliza Butterwhick,
a maid to the brothers Brown.

By day they preached propriety.
They fed the poor, but then,
by night they scurried underground,
those monsters dressed as men

Posters lined my work walk
of missing men and dames.
Children cried for parents lost,
yet none could find remains.

Whispers began brewing.
"The cemetery's looking full.
Black market stalls are flourishing,
and the poor have paid the toll."

I visited the graveyard
where plots had grown by eight
fresh dug graves without markers.
What had become their fates?

Behind me came a hissing.
I spun with such a fright.
I glimpsed a red-eyed woman
before she vanished out of sight.

Shaken, I rushed to the mansion
where the brothers demanded wine.
I served them in their dining hall
and searched for hidden signs.

Nothing seemed amiss that night.
They spoke of business deals.
I polished silver and listened close,
though nothing was revealed

until I stayed beyond my time.
I heard a bookcase groan.
I found a hidden passageway
marked by skull and bone.

I crept into the underground
that was deeper than a crypt.
I found them holding scalpels
over a body they had stripped.

"Her kidneys will buy us wine,"
one man cackled as he cut.
"Her heart will gain us land,
and fill our aching guts."

"We'll bury her," the other crowed.
"None will find her remains.
Then we'll peg our next victim
we endeavor to obtain."

With a gasp, I fled the scene.
Wait, did I hear a cry?
Had they seen me on the stairs?
Would I be next to die?

As I ran, I counted posters.
The missing equaled eight.
Were they the ones who were buried
behind the graveyard's gate?

I stepped onto that hallowed land
and counted up the mounds.
I knelt and dug into the dirt
until I was yanked around.

A stranger grabbed my wrist so tight
and flung me to the side.
"How dare you disturb her resting place?"
the red-eyed woman cried.

"I'm only searching for the truth,"
I said and scrambled back.
She advanced on me with pearly fangs,
poised to attack.

"I think I know who's killing folks
and burying them below.
Give me a chance to expose them
or the body count will grow."

The woman paused, suspicious,
as she crouched a foot away.
I realized then I'd never seen her
in the light of day.

"You think that you can trap them
when they've killed someone like me?
What can a little maid do
to set the secret free?"

I raised my chin, defiant.
"I'm stronger than I seem."
I told her of the hidden room
and the awful things I'd seen.

The woman nodded then and offered
a hand to help me up.
I grabbed her and released a gasp.
She was icy to the touch.

"They'll know that they were followed,"
she said and tapped her fang.
"You'll be next unless I help you."
Suddenly she sprang.

The next night when I went to work
and opened wide the door,
I took two steps and was knocked
down onto the hardwood floor.

My hands were bound behind me.
A kerchief gagged my lips.
More coils tied my ankles.
Someone grabbed my hips.

"We've caught our little spy,"
one brother sneered at me.
I was tossed over a shoulder,
unable to fight or flee.

They dropped me in a wagon
and praised their speed and skill
in preventing my escape
and revealing all their kills.

I heard an iron gate creak
and was hefted into arms
that bore me to the graveyard.
My heart leapt with alarm.

A brand-new hole stood gaping,
waiting to steal my youth.
They buried me on Sunday
because I'd learned the truth.

The dirt fell all around me.
It filled my nose, my eyes.
Worms crawled across my carcass.
The soil gagged my cries.

Earth shrouded me in darkness.
It weighed heavy on my chest.
I grasped a rock beneath me
and pressed it to my flesh.

They thought that they could kill me.
But what they didn't know—
I no longer needed air to breathe
while trapped down deep below.

My rock snipped through the fibers.
I raked hands through the dirt.
I clawed my way upward
and crawled out of the earth.

The brothers started shrieking.
They turned on heels to flee.
But the red-eye woman stopped them
and ushered them toward me.

Free of my bonds, I snickered.
I gave their cheeks a peck.
"You'll never hurt another soul."
I plunged fangs into their necks.

We fed upon the killers
then dropped them in my grave.
I kissed my red-eyed woman
for the gift she gave.

No one else goes missing.
We stroll the streets at night.
And when the killers beckon,
we destroy them with our bite.

Now we have our own crypt
where we tuck them safe and sound.
Beware the red-eyed women
who haunt the graveyard grounds.

Dark Waters
Jenn Patterson

Salcinaeum
Scott Alan Lewis

Claude Harper, April 28th, Expedition Day 1.

Linda-

I do not know when these pages will reach you as we are some distance from the nearest post. The expedition team is due to arrive on the 5th. I hope to send my correspondence with one of their supply runs. Regardless, I feel it necessary to record my experiences as well as my reasons for dragging our son across the continent on what is to him merely a camping expedition. You have long said that he and I would benefit from spending more time together. Hopefully this qualifies.

I truly believe this is the place. The location of Salcinaeum, the last great lost Roman city. Or at least the last until the next one. I do not presume to be the ultimate discoverer, though I hope to be an important one. I will not share my reasons for selecting this location on the chance that these missives will be intercepted. Save that for the papers I will one day write. Suffice it to say that we are deep in the mountains and far from the nearest village.

Jamie seems to like it here. He misses you terribly, of course, when he remembers to do so. He spent the hike up spotting animals and trying to run them down. Fortunately, the denizens of the Alps are agile enough to evade the most excitable of little boys, as I do not know what we would have done had he caught one. Like as not, I would have had to shoot it, and I daresay that would have ruined the poor lad's day. He is currently engaged in gathering our stock of firewood. I suspect that his process involves more rambling than carrying but as long as he is happy.

Tomorrow, we make our first excursion into the caves. I will not be able to do any sort of proper excavation until the team arrives, but I wanted to get here first and survey everything in its natural state before we tear it up. I say natural, though I'm not sure that's the word for a city buried by a volcano so thoroughly as to be lost to history. Pompeii and Herculaneum had, if not their survivors, then at least their witnesses. Salcinaeum was not so fortunate. I believe that the city was destroyed so suddenly and buried so deep that there wasn't anyone left to tell the story.

I'm sorry, I know you've heard all that before. I do go on. It's just that I am so close now. This is the site. Or it will be once we dig out the mountain that fell on the city. I can feel it. It has to be.

Jamie has returned form the trees, conspicuously lacking in firewood. I have promised him that I will not read what he writes to you if he practices his penmanship so brace yourself. More tomorrow, hopefully good news.

My love,
Claude

Hello mommy. I like the Alps. There aren't any kids here but I saw a goat. Daddy says it's a shammy but he was trying to fool me but I know what a goat looks like. Then it ran away. Daddy says if I'm brave I can go into the caves with him and look for his city. I hope there are kids there. Maybe next time we come to the Alps you can come with us and meet the shammy goat.

Claude Harper, April 29th, Expedition Day 2

Linda-

I am having some difficulty containing my excitement. My young assistant and I made an initial expedition into the caves today, and they were everything I had hoped. They wind for some distance into the mountain, further than we were willing to chart in a single day. Despite the depth they have proven easily navigable, so much so that I keep looking for signs that others have been here before me, but I find nothing. Only the entrance cave shows any sign of visitors and then only the four-legged sort. Jamie learned the word scat. He seems quite taken with it and for this I apologize.

When we delved past the entrance, it became clear that at least the geologic portion of my theory is correct. The rock strata are clearly from pyroclastic flow. There was a volcano here, and it was active sometime within the past few millennia. That alone is a find worth the trip, but I hold out for more. Sorry for the imprecision, but this is an initial survey. We will be able to date the eruption, or eruptions, with much greater precision once the team and their equipment arrive. Six days now. So little time to have the site to myself. Well, to ourselves, but I trust Jamie not to dig where he shouldn't or try to sneak his name onto my discovery. Discovery. The word makes me tingle.

Tomorrow, we go deeper. My plan is to take a single line through the cave and see how far down, and thus back in time, we can reach without undue risk. Neither of us are expert spelunkers, and while I might be willing to take a few chances with myself, I will not allow him to do so. Which means I can't allow myself to either. Lead by example and all that. Probably better this way. I do need to be here when the team arrives. It is likely too much to hope we'll make it down to Roman layers tomorrow, but given how navigable, and dare I say welcoming, the caves seem, I hold out some small hope. Jamie seems to be enjoying himself. He was very brave his first time in the cave. Indeed, he has taken to the place. When we were making our way out, I confess to being a bit turned around. Sometimes it seems as though the passages move about when you aren't looking. Not so Jamie. "That one goes out Daddy" he said to me, sure as anything. And so it did. We may have a budding caver on our hands.

My love,
Claude

I like caves Mommy. Daddy said it would be dark and scary and he gave me my own lantern to carry but it wasn't scary at all. It was fun. We got to climb over things and crawl around on rocks and the cave talks to you. It goes drip and woosh and mostly rumble. I told Daddy I wanted to call the cave Mr. Rumbles but he said it already had a name and I was being silly. I wasn't being silly. I love you Mommy.
- Jamie

Claude Harper, April 30th, Expedition Day 3

Linda-

Spot of drama in the caves today. I was in one of the larger caverns extracting rock samples and working on my sketches when I noticed Jamie had wandered off from where he had been piling up loose rocks. I called to him from all of the exits, but he did not respond. I admit I panicked a bit before reason took over, and I thought to shutter my lamp. I could just make out the light from his lantern coming from a downward sloping passage that we had not yet explored. Well, I hadn't. It seems our little caver is already mounting his own expeditions.

It took several minutes of twists and turns to follow the light to its source. I had to wedge myself through a passage that made me feel both my age and weight, then scramble down a patch of loose gravel. I swear his lantern was moving away from me no matter how I called.

When I found him, he was buried to his chest in a pile of rocks. I have no idea how he got in there. They didn't fall on him, or if they did, they somehow managed to do so without injuring a fragile little boy. He wasn't scared. No. He was laughing and chattering away to no one in particular. He didn't even respond to me until I grabbed him by the arm, and then it was just "Hi daddy." I'm afraid I may have raised my voice to the boy. I certainly dragged him all the way out of the cave and back to camp. Left him there in a furious pout under orders not to come back into the caves anymore.

No real progress today beyond mapmaking. Between the lost work in tracking him down and the furor in which it put me, I'm afraid I was of little use to anyone. When I got back to my work site, my equipment was scattered about the cavern. Some freak wind through the caves, or perhaps I did some of it when I first realized Jamie was missing. Worse yet, on my way back out of the cavern I got lost. Me, who has been doing this sort of thing for more years than I care to admit. I took a wrong turn coming out of a set of caves I've been through half a dozen times already and whose layout I have put to paper. I was so flustered I could accomplish nothing more than to scrabble together our dinner and shuffle my notes listlessly for the remainder of the evening.

I have asked Jamie whether he wishes to write to you this evening. I take from his response that he is not currently speaking to me, so if there are no more words you may presume that that, like all the ills of the world, is my fault.

My Love,
Claude

I made a friend today. He said he likes being called Mr. Rumbles and we played all over the caves but then Father came and yelled at us and said I can't go back. He is mean and stinky and all he ever talks about is his city full of dead people. He isn't ever going to find them unless he lets us play.

Claude Harper, May 1st, Expedition Day 4

Linda-

All is forgiven between Jamie and I, for your intrepid adventurers have made a great discovery. This morning while we were cleaning up breakfast, I raised the question of whether Jamie would be able to remain nearby if I were to allow him to accompany me back into the cave. He began to babble on about meeting someone in the cave and how he had to go back and see whoever it was. I was just about to lecture him on being a serious young man and not inventing playmates, but then he said his friend took him to a place "where the dead people keep their dishes." Out of the mouths of babes. He described the place, and I must admit that all thought of past transgressions fled from my mind. Somehow, in his ill-advised wanderings Jamie had stumbled upon evidence of a prior settlement precisely where I had hoped to find one. My mind lept to Salcinaeum, but I forced myself to remember that I am an academic, not a fantasist. Time enough for conclusions after the site had been documented and analyzed. Won't the team be surprised when they arrive to find the first half of the work done for them?

We abandoned any pretense of doing dishes. I gathered up my sketch
pad and we made haste back to the cave entrance. Today there were no
wrong turns. I went directly back to the cavern where Jamie and I got
separated yesterday. From there I let him take the lead. He seemed
uncertain at first, almost as though he was talking it over with himself.
Then he took off. He wasn't quite running, but if we weren't in a cave, I
think he would have been. He seemed almost possessed. We went down,
back up and down again, through caves and passages for I know not
how long. I tried as best I could to keep pace and take enough notes that
we would be able to return. At one point I was sure we passed by the
place I found him yesterday. I called to Jamie to slow down but he was
so far ahead of me that it was all I could do just to keep up. I was on
the verge of halting with or without him when we found it.

Not a cave. That word is too small. A cavern and at the same time a
capsule. Salcinaeum. Part of it anyway. Buildings intact enough to
speculate at their purpose. Remains of unfortunates who must have been
caught in the eruption. Linda, today I walked down a Roman street. I
believe I am the first man to have done so since it was in use. I am glad
the team was not there to see my initial reaction, as it was less than
dignified. I confess I behaved as something of a tourist. I wandered the
galleries of Salcinaeum and simply saw. Meanwhile Jamie played in the
streets after my admonishment not to disturb any of the buildings.

After a time even this most extreme novelty wore off, and I set to work.
I sketched a layout of the place and a sampling of its contents. Then I
unpacked our lunch, eaten in what I believe to have been a common
outdoor dining facility, and began to make notes on what might have
happened here. Reading back over them tonight each idea seems more
far-fetched than the last. How could a section of city have been
preserved under the earth, when the earth rising up and burying the city is
what destroyed it? The cavern has a vaulted roof which might have
shielded them from the tremors, but that roof would not have been
there until after the city was buried. So how did I see structures intact,
people paused as though they dropped in place? I do not know. It may
be the work of a lifetime to find out. I hope to bring you here someday.
To see this great place that will forever be associated with our name.

I would gladly have kept working until I was no longer able to stand. If
I had been alone, I would likely have spent the night in some adjacent

cave. Jamie was of a very different mind. After some hours he began to grow restless. Twice he came to where I was working and said we had to leave. The first time I brushed him off as one does a child, with vague promises of leaving soon. I regretted it shortly after, remembering how I felt when so treated. With that in mind I took him more seriously on the second occasion, asking him why we had to leave this wondrous place. He said, "because we aren't welcome here anymore" and then repeated his insistence that we leave now. I responded that the residents weren't in any shape to protest our presence, but as he looked on the verge of tears, I relented. There will be time, after all. I saw no reason to do the boy harm for the sake of my haste.

As we left the cavern of Salcinaeum and passed through the cave complex, I tried to connect my previous notes so that I could get the route down, lest our memory slip on the morrow. I found the distance between each observation shorter than I recalled, and indeed the entire trip out seemed to take barely half the time as the trip in. I suppose that is the effect of a lighter heart. For his part Jamie seemed overjoyed when we escaped the place that, just this morning, he had been on the edge of tantrum over being denied.

I had intended for his accompanying me on this trip to bring us closer together. It seems to have had the opposite effect. We are ever at cross purposes. When I say stay, he goes. When I lag behind, he runs ahead. Where I find greatness, he trembles in fear. We fought again, this time over our plans for tomorrow. I am, of course, going to return to the cavern of Salcinaeum. I can imagine no other course. Jamie is near collapse at the idea. He keeps ranting that we are not welcome and that we can't go to where the dead people live. He goes on about how someone called Mr. Rumbles won't like it. Damndest thing of it is when he was at his loudest, most squalling about the matter, I swear I felt a small tremor. My imagination certainly combined with the stress of both discovery and managing a mercurial little boy.

I have made it quite clear that I will be returning in the morning. Whether he comes along or remains at camp is his choice, and though it pains me to say it, I rather hope he chooses to stay here. There is so much to discover, and I will do better work if I am not distracted by making sure he does not run off ever deeper into the earth. He is entombed in his sleeping roll right now, shaking slightly. I think he might be sobbing. Best to let him work it out of his system. I don't think he will have anything to add to today's message. I will speak to him again in the morning when hopefully we will both be in better sorts. One thing is certain though. Whether the dead welcome me or not, I am going back to Salcinaeum, and I will tell its story.

Claude Harper, May 2nd, Expedition Day 5

Claude Harper, May 3rd, Expedition Day 6

Claude Harper, May 4th, Expedition Day 7

I'm sorry mommy. I'm sorry. Mr. Rumbles made me do it. He said I had to and now he says I have to go back and hide with the dead people. I'm sorry mommy. I love you. I'm sorry.

The Lovers
Nana Abuladze

To L.

It is said that you're not a real Iowan, until a deer runs into your car

We are two does at the highway,
Under the red maple
Which is now black, dressed in night.
You see the fierce light,
But you – troubled and terrified –
Cross the road regardless.
And I
Follow you,
Since the deer always go in pairs.
Your graceful leap in the air –
My last view
Before night
Falls in my eyes,
Before light
Embraces me.

Oh, Earth,
Our Mother,
I beg you,
Guard her and guide her
Wherever she goes.
Oh, Earth,
Our Mother,
I beg you,
Guard her and guide her
Wherever she goes.
Oh, Earth,
Our Mother,
I
Beg
You...

Nature Doesn't Respect You
Spike Dawkins

Gaia
Jill Cronbaugh

Mid-March, Northern Hemisphere

Brad tapped his toes as he gave the sweaty, frantically gyrating crowd a once-over before he turned his attention back to his girlfriend of the moment and whatever it was she was whining about now.

"Yeah, sure, babe."

"You haven't heard a word I said, have you, you prick?!" To his utter disgust, she burst into tears.

"Okay. You're right. What were you saying?"

"Have you been sleeping with Sherri?"

Here we go, thought Brad. It's been a great time, but whattya gonna do?

"Oh. That. Yeah. She's got a great ass. You've got a great rack. Together, you're the perfect woman."

Surprisingly, she broke into a deep gut-level laugh. "Joke's on you asshole! She's pregnant. And so am I!"

Brad blanked for a moment, then his innate personality recovered. "Well, you can both get that taken care of across state lines. If you need gas money, hit me up."

With her stunned silence, he assumed the conversation was over and continued to scan the crowd of dancers. The music morphed into a slow, pulsating groove. The bulk of the frenetic dancers left the floor for a break. In the center of the grinding couples was a woman. Brad sat up and stared.

To his predatorial eye, she was not model-perfect, which made her ultimately attainable. She was lithe yet voluptuous in the way that old movie stars were. What was that woman's name? Oh yeah, the woman sinuously gyrating on the dance floor reminded him of the Italian babe in that old circus movie Sherri made him watch two weeks ago. Gina something or other. Brad shook his head, whipping his blond hair into his face. Didn't matter what the old bitch's name was. This woman was one he could fuck into next month.

"Brad!" The ex shrieked into his ear. Christ. Was she still here? Brad ignored the enraged crying until she slapped him square in his face. Without thinking, he backhanded her off the stool.

One burly bouncer in a too-small bar shirt picked her up and asked her if she was okay. She slapped at his hands so he released her and watched as she stormed out of the bar.

"Not cool, man. Only reason you're not tossed out the fuckin' door is I saw her roundhouse you first. Still a shitass move. I'll be watching you."

Brad flipped off the bouncer and went back to the woman. Hands high above her head twirling and rotating at her wrists, her nicely muscled arms glistened with a fine sheen of sweat. Her eyes were closed and her face emitted a quiet, almost reverent, joy in her movement to the music. The heavy spheres of her breasts, lifted by her raised arms, gently moved to the rhythm of her abdomen rolling in and out like the tide. Full, tapered hips accompanied a beautifully tight, round ass as she swayed and undulated. Long legs that laughed at the idea of thigh gaps anchored her to the ground and provided the pivot point for her sensual swirling. Brad blinked at her blush pink-manicured bare feet, but then his eyes snapped back to her midsection.

The tempo rushed to the end of the song and her arms opened wide. Wavy brown mane of hair flowed from the crown of her rapturously thrown-back head as she spun faster and faster. Her abrupt stop startled Brad out of his reverie. Her arms still thrown open, she stood still as a plinth. Her head raised slowly and she opened her eyes. Deep brown wells burrowed into Brad's soul.

He came back to himself as she blinked and turned to the bar. Slipping her feet into woven, open-toed wedges, she slid onto the bar stool and smilingly nodded her thanks to the bartender for the glass of iced clear liquid placed next to her hand.

Brad stood and adjusted the uncomfortably tight crotch of his jeans. With a slight roll of his shoulders and a quick crack of his neck, he was ready to engage her with "the approach."

Propping his hip on the barstool next to her, he spread his legs, ostensibly to brace himself, but he knew this opened his thighs and pulled his jeans taut across his impressive package. If she was the kind of woman that noticed this, he'd have a better than even chance of bagging her tonight. If she wasn't—no blood, no foul. There were other tried and true moves to make. He rapped the bar for attention and signaled the bartender. Another beer appeared at his elbow.

Brad patiently stared at her ear. He noticed her skin was deep golden-brown and smooth. So finely textured that he couldn't see any pores at all. He wanted to reach out a finger and stroke her cheek to see if she was wearing artful makeup. He'd been with many a woman whose face underwent more than subtle changes after a morning wash.

She turned her head to him just as he realized his hand was reaching toward her face. He quickly yanked his hand to his hip and gave her his most charming grin.

"I'm Brad. That was incredible. You've got to be thirsty. Let me get your next round in appreciation of that dance."

Her eyes focused through his to the back of his head. He almost felt naked, but since that was the direction he wanted to go with her, he was comfortable with it. He wasn't exactly sure how long their eye-lock took, but when she inclined her head in assent, he could smell victory.

She sipped her drink in silence as he presented her with his best material. He couldn't tell if any of it was landing, but she hadn't slapped him or walked away, so he rolled on with it. When she finished the drink he got for her, she turned her head toward him again. After a very thoughtful gaze, she leaned toward him and stabilized herself with a hand to his thigh. Her cheek next to his, she steadily inhaled. Still as stone, Brad held his breath, intrigued by her behavior.

Pulling back, her eyes warmed for the first time and she slid off the barstool. Her gently swaying hips riveted his attention as she slowly undulated toward the exit. His rapt scrutiny broke when she turned to him and cocked her eyebrow inquisitively. She continued to the door without looking back to see if he was following.

Brad scrambled from his stool and threw a handful of bills to the bartender. "Keep the change!" He caught up to her just as she crossed the threshold into the cool spring night.

Brad continued to chat as he followed her through the darkened streets. Occasional streetlights created spotlit areas on the cracked sidewalk. She continued at a determined but leisurely pace. She provided no answers to any of his questions or any recognition of his presence. At first, Brad relished this about her; most women he had anything to do with couldn't stop talking to him - as if he cared about anything going on in their heads. But then, he started to feel ignored, looked down on even.

Brad grabbed her arm and spun her to face him in the weak spotlight. He got his first real look at her face. He was mesmerized by her deep brown eyes and light dusting of freckles across her rounded pug-nose. Her full, deep crimson lips were slightly parted, revealing even, ivory-white teeth. He blinked and his anger returned.

"You think you're too good to talk to me?! What's with you?

You mute? I asked you what your name is. You can tell me that, at the very least!"

Her eyes briefly flashed gold as her lips turned up so very slightly that he thought he might be imagining it all, but then he heard her voice. So husky and feminine, he immediately got rock hard.

"Gaia."

Stunned, he released her arm and she turned to continue her glide toward the end of the block. Quickly stumbling to catch up with her, he wondered if he actually saw her lips move. Shaking his head, he realized it didn't even matter. He had to have this woman. Tonight. Nothing short of his death would stop him.

The sporadic streetlights petered out as she led him through one of the sketchiest neighborhoods in town. The pitch black night was relieved only by the preternaturally bright full moon.

Just when he thought she'd been leading him to some sort of ambush robbery, she stopped. He was surprised to see an empty lot.

"Isn't this one of those areas where they're trying to make a fucking community garden or some such shit? I heard it's so toxic they can't get anything to grow. The hell we doin' here?"

She actually looked at him then and smiled gently. Reaching her hand to him, he eagerly clutched at her. She came close enough for him to smell her. Ah god! Fresh cut grass, apples, wet black earth, and musk. He'd never had anything smell so good before.

She kicked off her shoes and led him into the lot. His brain started to protest and was cut down brutally by his dick. Hard didn't even come close. He was made of diamond, titanium, adamant. He could fuck every woman in the world and go for a second round!

Her warm hand in his was all he could feel. She pulled him to the center of the lot and then down to the ground. His clothes miraculously disappeared and he knelt between her legs. Sinking his face into her neck, her scent enveloped him. As he breathed heavily and nipped her neck below her ear, her entire body jerked. Encouraged, he licked and kissed his way across her collarbone. Lifting and gently squeezing her breasts together, her nipples presented an irresistible target for his teeth. Her low moan inflamed him as her arms reached around him to grasp his buttocks and pull him into her.

"Aaaaaah...." his moaning sigh echoed across the empty lot. She was wet and so warm she almost burned him. Her heels gently rode him, spurring him on to deeper and faster thrusts. He could feel his lifejuice building in his balls and at the base of his spine.

She pulled her head up to gently place her lips on his as she slowly melted into soft, black, loamy soil. Still pumping furiously, he was horrified to find he could not stop, nor could he pull out or back. He thrust and thrust into the cooling soil until the volcanic rush of cum started to spurt madly. Each sputtering thrust pushed him farther and farther into the soft soil until all that was left were the faint mounds of dark dirt resembling his naked ass.

Mid-June, Northern Hemisphere

"Mama, Mama! Come look!"

Small, brown hands pulled a heavily gravid woman to the center of an urban jungle.

"Look how big my lettuces is!"

"I see, baby. They're purt near as big as you!"

"I told you! I told you this was a good lot!"

"You surely did. How'd you know, sweetie?"

"I prayed to Mama Nature, just like Gran told me about. For months and months. She musta heared me and says, what a good child you are, you should have good food to eat!"

The Garden Plot
Nicholas Lee

Vi, Vi, Vi. I did it. I know I've been saying I would since before we moved in. It's taken a while, but we both know I've had a lot of time on my hands. Out back are a shovel, soil, and miscellaneous garden supplies. Don't you love that word, "miscellaneous?" The man at the greenhouse said it was the best soil for miscellaneous growing, for decorative and functional plants, the brassicas, the broccoli, the basil, all in good thyme. Will you always laugh at my bon mots, your little buffoon? I bought another croissant from the Frenchman. I hold out hope I will develop a taste for their authenticity, but I guess my heart still belongs to Pillsbury. I will start digging tomorrow. By the time you get back, you'll have a good base to start from at least. I'll take care of the dirty work. What's a little slice of earth, a crumb of crust? I wish I could give you the world.

***

Didn't start digging yet. I stayed in bed most of the day.

***

Broke ground today! I didn't expect buried treasure. It has been humid today, but I hate being behind schedule. I only got a couple of feet before I hit something solid. "Got a" is "toga" backwards, and that's the only interesting thing about it. Such a vulgar phrase, in both senses, useful for its invisibility but hard on the ear, a guttural attack, the worst of the Anglo-Saxon utterances.

My buried treasure consists of no jewels nor dubloons, but I did find sturdy banker's boxes. They're not a climate-controlled method of preservation, but they were freshly buried enough that their deterioration was minimal. I don't think they belonged to the previous owner, but how can you tell who has an obsessive interest in true crime? We've watched plenty of Dateline ourselves, and I love my Capote. You have your Christie.

I broke ground at sixish and made it about three feet before the thud. Okay, it was more of a thwap. Three boxes: one of periodicals and clippings, one of multimedia, and one of files. The files look rather official. I wonder where they got them from. Oh, no. I have a "they" now.

***

I didn't get to the garden today. The university called. They wanted some records and some questions answered. I'm not sure why I acquiesced. It made me feel useful, I suppose. Then there were the boxes. I started with the periodicals. Since I was a boy in the library, learning the card catalog, I have loved periodicals. They're a dying form, I know. Secondary sources are the best entry point to a new research endeavor. Perhaps I'll do a literature review. I haven't come to the part where you learn why she did it, or maybe what he did to deserve it. She went Lizzie Borden on him! She stabbed him thirty-seven times and buried him in the backyard. She said it was in self-defense. In my experience, limited as it is, the police lend less credence to a story of self-defense when the stab wounds reach the double digits, especially when some of them are in the back.

***

I jumped the gun and started looking at the online posts. Who prints off web pages anymore? The same people who bury salacious crime research in their backyard, that's who.

I was looking at the seed catalog as well. We could grow some tomatoes, potatoes, eggplants, and rhubarb. For flowers, I was thinking poinsettias, rhododendrons, monkshood, and violets, of course. I thought about some hot peppers as well, for me. You can't handle anything warmer than a jalapeno. I should do this later. If I don't hurry up, the plot won't be filled before you get back.

***

Killer Murders Dot Com -- "Woman, 45, Stabs Husband, 52, 37 Times" -- 10 replies

Nightstalk66: See this one yet? Do you buy this self-defense crap?

Tedsgurl: ***believewomen

Nightstalk66: I do! Usually. But she buried him in the backyard,

76

dude! And stabbed him 37 times!

Tedsgurl: Traumatic events put you into shock. Victims don't always act rational. She was probably scared he'd attack her again. You can't trust the police. ***acab

Nightstalk66: Uh, I'm pretty sure he was dead by the time she buried him. It's not like he could hurt her. You're right about the cops, but still. It doesn't look like self-defense to moi.

Tedsgurl: Trauma doesn't have a time limit.

Nightstalk66: I know that. Are you telling me you think it's really the most likely explanation, though?

HerculeParrot: Tedsgurl is a known troll. I swear they're some kind of plant trying to discredit survivors. Fucking fascists.

Tedsgurl: TEDSGURL WAS BANNED FOR THIS POST.

Nightstalk66: I believe women and support survivors!

HerculeParrot: *raises fist* Right on!

***

You'll never guess who emailed me. Victor Lance, author of seminal works in the field. My field. The bastard. He offered his support and condolences. I keep getting these from other academics, the cowards. They're too craven to support me in public, but they'll believe in cancel culture once it happens to them.

That's another good word. Seminal and semen come from the same root, from a word for seed, which is etymologically related itself. Did you know my old office was in the old seminary building? This was before we met. I liked to think I was planting a new crop of thinkers every year, that I was introducing them to a larger world of thought, sowing their minds as it were. Now I'm picking out literal seeds. They come in these little envelopes, just like the ones when I was a boy. The names are more interesting now: Slipstream Tomatoes, Vampire Eggplants, Aristotelian Potatoes. I can't believe these prices. No wonder the farmer's market has gotten so expensive. Maybe I'll dig a few more plots and make some money back. I could retire my way into a new career.

***

Initial Interview -- Suspect: Morgenshtern -- Detective Richard Katz -- 04/12/2011 -- 08:11 PM

Katz: Would you like some coffee?

Morgenshtern: No. Thank you.

Katz: Water?

Morgenshtern: No.

Katz: Quite the mess, isn't it?

48 seconds of silence

Katz: Did he hit you?

23 seconds of silence

Katz: Cheat on you?

12 seconds of silence

Katz: Did he --

Morgenshtern: He was going to kill me.

Katz: How do you know?

silence for 102 seconds

Katz: When did this happen?

Morgenshtern: It was in May, a Friday I think. He got home after midnight. He was drunk. I knew he had women on the side. You saw the news. Everyone did. I told him I was leaving him and would take him for all he was worth.

Katz: I bet he didn't like that.

Morgenshtern: No. He got really quiet. Then he went to the kitchen. He came back with a knife.

Katz: This knife?

Morgenshtern: I said something stupid like, "What are you going to do with that?" He lunged at me and tripped over the ottoman. It's this ratty old brown faux leather thing. I was always vacuuming up little flakes from it.

Katz: I have a chair like that. My wife hates it.

Morgenshtern: I feel her pain. Anyway, the knife is lying there at my feet.

Katz: You didn't try to run?

Morgenshtern: He was getting up. He was between me and the door. So I picked up the knife. I tried to run past him, honestly, but he grabbed me. Next thing I know he's on the floor, bleeding.

***

From "The Altars of Bitter Gods" by Joseph Salicin

The podunk town of Shibboleth lies prostrate, deep in barley country, far out in the boonies as the locals say. As placid as fleeced lambs, they leave their windows open with pies on the windowsills in the summer, and door-to-door alarm salesmen know not to stop there for more than gas and a stack of pancakes.

It was March 2, 2011. Allison Jane had moved into the lavender blue house less than a year prior. The garden out back was well-stocked when she moved in -- tomatoes and potatoes, eggplants and rhubarb, poinsettias and monkshood, and violets. She decided this year to replace the eggplants with tomatillos.

"I was in the garden. It was about 1:11 PM. I remember because I was wearing a watch in those days. My husband -- this was a couple of years before my great lesbian revelation and subsequent late blooming -- comes out with a pitbull on a leash. I could've killed him. I had told him no dog but definitely not a pitbull of all things. Anyway, we had a hell of a row, probably entertained Mrs. Jankes. She kept tabs on everyone. We went inside after a while and left the dog outside. Sure enough, by the time he remembered the creature, it had dug a big hole out there. It had a big, long bone in its mouth, a dirty one with little bits still attached. I didn't know what I was looking at first."

The story made waves in the local news, all the way up to the state level, a lot for such a little college town. It made less than a blip nationally -- too few bodies for a start -- but for a community whose last murder was a decade prior, the story would become ingrained in local lore and probably will remain there for a lifetime if not more.

According to Morgenshtern's account, her husband arrived home that night after 12:00 AM. He'd been drinking, and she accused him of meeting a girlfriend that night. He denied it, and she told him she was leaving him. Allegedly, he then went to the kitchen and shortly returned with a long knife. He lunged at her but tripped over an ottoman, and the knife landed near her feet. He suffered a projected thirty-seven stab wounds. Due to the advanced state of decomposition when the body was discovered, inspectors extrapolated this number from marks on the skeleton, clothing, and knife itself, which was buried with the body.

The prosecution argued that Morgenshtern harbored resentment over the humiliation she experienced due to her husband's recent scandal and resignation from his position at St. Lepus University. There was also a financial motive. Her husband was a respected academic but had little in the way of means, and she faced the prospect of supporting him from then on.

A significant amount of speculation arose over the matter of the professor's disappearance and its handling at the time. Records show the police never investigated Morgenshtern before the discovery of the body months later. Typically, police will investigate a romantic partner in such a case. Prior to putting the house on the market, itself a lightning fast sale, she replaced the hardwood floor with carpet. Subsequent analysis showed traces of the victim's blood on the wood, and the blood left a trail consistent with the prosecution's assertion that the professor crawled twenty feet toward the backyard door and passed out on the threshold. The defense argued that Morgenshtern had dragged the body the whole way. This was an important detail because the prosecution argued she had known the professor was alive when she started shoveling soil on him.

Morgenshtern was found not guilty of murder. As for why she wasn't investigated sooner, the people of Shibboleth were perhaps disinterested in the professor's story and even glad to be rid of him. Before the murder revelation, his scandal was the greatest source of shame the community had faced in some time. They were more willing to accept the lie that the earth had swallowed me.

***

I'm sorry for what I put you through, Vi. I thought I could start to make it up to you. I could endure my banishment, the shunning by my peers. I could endure the judgment of strangers. I could never bear the shadow of your face turned away from me, not the cold of that slope of Erebus.

***

Initial Interview -- Violet Morgenshtern -- Detective Richard Katz -- 04/12/2011 -- 08:11 PM

Katz: Would you like some coffee?
Morgenshtern: No. Thank you.
Katz: Water?
Morgenshtern: No.
Katz: Quite the mess, isn't it?
48 seconds of silence
Katz: Did he hit you?
23 seconds of silence
Katz: Cheat on you?
12 seconds of silence
Katz: Did he --
Morgenshtern: He was going to kill me.

Katz: How do you know?

silence for 102 seconds

Katz: When did this happen?

Morgenshtern: It was in May, a Friday I -- Joseph? What are you -- how?

Salicin: No more lies, Violet.

Katz: How did you get in here? What are you doing?

Joseph pushed the detective, and the younger man fell backwards over the folding chair, which clattered onto the floor. Joseph picked up the evidence bag and took out the knife. Detective Katz rose and grabbed his wrist, and Joseph slashed the detective's throat. A crimson geyser erupted from the policeman's carotid artery. Violet screamed. She ran past the struggling men, opened the door of the interrogation room, and stepped through.

***

Vi, Vi, Vi. I did it. I know I've been saying I would since before we moved in. It's taken a while, but we both know I've had a lot of time on my hands. Out back are a shovel, soil, and miscellaneous garden supplies. Don't you love that word, "miscellaneous?" The man at the store said it was the best soil for miscellaneous growing, for decorative and functional plants, the brassicas, the broccoli, the basil, all in good thyme. Will you always laugh at my bon mots, your little buffoon? I bought another croissant from the Frenchman. I hold out hope I will develop a taste for their authenticity, but I guess my heart still belongs to Pillsbury. I will start digging tomorrow. By the time you get back, you'll have a good base to start from at least. I'll take care of the dirty job. What's a little slice of earth, a crumb of crust? I wish I could give you the world. Now that you're here, I can.

Violet stood in the study of the house she'd lived in with her husband. Professor Joseph Salicin sat at his typewriter. He was middle-aged with a hawk-nose and salt-and-pepper hair. His eyes were wet when he said, "I've been working in the garden, getting it ready for you. Just the way you wanted."

Violet backed up. She wore a long red dress. She was just a

notch above plain, with eyes only a trifle too close together. Her back touched a bookshelf. The rough cloth of the antique hardbacks pressed into the nape of her neck.

"What are you going to do with that, Joe?" she asked.

"Nothing," he said. He still held the knife. "If you forgive me, I'll forgive you. We can go back to the way things were, except it'll just be the two of us. We can work in the garden. Go to the theater. Like the best times."

She bowed her head a little. "Just the two of us?"

"That's right." He smiled with nascent ecstasy and dropped the knife on the desk. She walked to him, and they embraced. He closed his eyes and buried his face in her neck. She rubbed his back with her left hand and picked up the knife with her right.

***

Violet dumped the last shovel of dirt on the plot and patted it flat. She sighed at all the seeds. "I'll have to get some starters. It's too late for these, you idiot, and I hate violets." As she walked over the threshold and into the house, she said, "But thanks for doing the dirty work."

.

Dirt, Clay, Bricks
Spike Dawkins

Contributors

Jordan Cronbaugh (she/her) is a Des Moines area-based artist who enjoys writing poetry and taking photos in her spare time. Her other loves include the social sciences and her dog; she received her BA in Psychology in 2019 and her MA in Counseling in 2022.

Madeleine Kleppinger (she/her) spends her nights as a lab manager, and her days writing. Her written works include Chimes, published articles on Scribbler and 50-Word stories, and a blog (www.mkleppinger.com) for helping readers discover their greatest story. Find her any day with a fresh carafe of coffee, a table full of people, and Sonnet her American Bulldog.

Spike Dawkins (she/her) is the pen name of a crime and horror novelist and photographer. Her novel, Lost Boys, was shortlisted for the Crime Writers' Association Debut Dagger Award in 2017. She lives in Iowa City.

Diane DeBok (she/her) has a B.A. in English from Simpson College and is an editor and content manager at the University of Iowa. She lives in Riverside with her husband Bruce. She is also a member of Washington County Master Gardeners.

Dennis Maulsby's (he/him) poems and short stories have appeared in *The North American Review, Star*Line, The Hawai'i Pacific Review, The Briarcliff Review (Pushcart nomination),* and on National Public Radio's *Themes & Variations.* His published books include *Near Death/ Near Life, Free Fire Zone, Winterset, Heart Songs,* and *House de Gracie.* Website: www.dennismaulsby.com.

Erin Casey (she/her) is an urban fantasy writer and author of The Purple Door District series. She's a Founder of The Writers' Rooms. An advocate for mental health, she openly talks about her struggles with depression/anxiety on her social media platforms. Visit erincasey.org to learn more.

Rachel J. Sharkey (she/her) has returned home to Calgary, Alberta, Canada, but still visits The Writers' Rooms in Iowa digitally via the powers of Zoom.

Trevor Yurek (he/him) graduated from the University of Iowa in 2021 with a degree in finance and certificate in writing. He is now an accountant for the same university in the Department of Anatomy and Cell Biology. He enjoys writing poetry and the occasional short story in his free time.

Nicholas Lee (he/him) A writer and game designer, Nick lives in Iowa City with a rabbit. Nick harbors a suspicion that this world is not the one they grew up in.

J.E. Brooke (she/her) is an anthropologist by day, science fiction and fantasy writer by night. When she isn't writing stories and novels, she can be found knitting or cross stitching nerdy things, experimenting with her sourdough starter, or lost in the pages of a good book.

R. R. Brown (he/him) is a writer, long-distance cyclist, and aspiring ski-bum who lives in America's heartland.

Mike Keller-Wilson (he/him) lives, writes, and teaches in Iowa City, Iowa. He is a founder & co-editor-in-chief of Vast Chasm Magazine. In his day job, he teaches writing and dad jokes to a captive audience of 7th graders. Find him on Twitter @Mike3Stars or at mikekellerwilson.com.

Jenn Patterson (she/they): Since 2010, Jenn has found much joy in letting a painting or photo become whatever it wants to be. Jenn has raised over $2,000 for local nonprofits by auctioning their artwork. "Dark Waters" is an edited photo of an acrylic painting splashed with water, evoking a stormy, unearthly terrain.

Scott Alan Lewis (he/him) is a financial analyst and itinerant gamer who writes to give the demons an outlet and manages the stage combat company Rage Theatrics in case the writing isn't enough for them. Scott lives in a 90 year old Moffit house with his partner and two cats.

Nana Abuladze (she/her) is a fiction writer and literary scholar from Tbilisi, Georgia and the author of two books: "Akumi," and"The New Perception (A Mass for Women Soloists and a Mixed Choir)." Her stay in the US inspired her to write her first poems in English: "The Lovers" and "The Water Tower".

Jill Cronbaugh (she/her) hates writing author bios. Her first piece was a short-story at the age of 6 about the time her grandpa took her to steal some field corn for her pony. The reviews were great! It delighted her grandfather & embarrassed her mother –- all-in-all, a job well done!

ALSO CHECK OUT
THE WRITERS' ROOMS

the writers' rooms
www.TheWritersRooms.org

OUR ROOTS

The Writers' Rooms began in late 2015 under the welcoming umbrella of the Iowa Writers' House. We had a simple mission in mind: create a free, accessible community to Iowan writers. The Violet Realm, our sci-fi/fantasy Room, started it all. For two years we incubated under the IWH and learned what our community needed to foster creative minds. It became apparent that if we were going to support our writers, it would be through a community- and crowd-sourced endeavor.

OUR MISSION

Our writing community has the amazing benefit of a massive collection of backgrounds, experiences, and viewpoints. The Writers' Rooms endeavors to bring these wonderful ideas together and help all writers with their craft. We strive to encourage and foster community-based knowledge to help lead literary sessions and provide a safe, positive writing environment. Our Rooms are moderated by both our Concierges and the members of our community. Community-led sessions tap into the wealth of our collective knowledge, allowing our writers to both share their own experiences and learn from other attendees.

The Rooms can't exist without you and your passion and experience!

OUR PEOPLE
Concierge members come from the writing community. All of our current concierges were interested in their topics and became knowledgeable about their genre through reading, writing, and taking lessons of their own. Anyone interested in leading a particular genre- or topic-based Room is welcome to e-mail us at welcome@thewritersrooms.org.

The rest of the Room membership comes from eager writer minds who want to know more about a particular genre or topic. Some have even graciously led lessons for us. We're always looking for more people to share their expertise.

Find out more at: Facebook (IAWritersRooms),
and follow us on Instagram (@WritersRooms)
and Twitter (@IAWritersRooms).

Donations

The Writers' Rooms are and will always be free to the public.
Everything we do is out-of-pocket from our Director and Concierges,
funded by the sale of anthologies and merchandise, or the product of
generous donations from the community.
All proceeds are used wholly for The Writers' Rooms' day-to-day
operational expenses, to fund event appearances and community
outreach, and to publish our annual Community Anthology.

Donate through…
PayPal! www.Paypal.me/thewritersrooms
CashApp! www.cash.app/$thewritersrooms
Ko-fi! www.Ko-fi.com/thewritersrooms

Purchase our Anthologies! www.thewritersrooms.org/store
Prefer eBooks? All of our anthologies (A New Adventure, Writers of
the Depths, and Writers of the Aether, Writers of the Flame, Writers of
the Loam) are available for purchase on our website.

Check out our Teespring! www.the-writers-rooms.creator-spring.com
Here you can buy a host of different items from The Writers' Rooms
and specific Rooms, like our TWR Pride shirt or Make It Gay mug!
Not seeing something you want? Submit a request to
welcome@thewritersrooms.org!

Subscribe to our Patreon! www.patreon.com/TheWritersRooms
This subscription service allows you to support The Writers' Rooms on a
monthly basis, for as little as $1 per month. You will be featured on our
Donate page at
www.thewritersrooms.org/donate. Keep an eye out for more Patron
perks soon!

Thank you! We can't do this without you!

www.ingramcontent.com/pod-product-compliance
Lightning Source LLC
Chambersburg PA
CBHW031309130726
47988CB00007B/2783